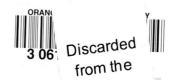

AUGER

Artist: Francine Auger

John G. Diefenbaker, 1895-1979.

Arthur Slade

Arthur Slade is the author of four books for young adults: *Draugr*, which was nominated for a Saskatchewan Book Award for Children and a Small Press Book Award in the U.S., *The Haunting of Drang Island*, *The Loki Wolf*, and *Dust*. He also penned the comic book *Hallowed Knight*, which was made in Saskatchewan and sold worldwide. His short fiction and non-fiction work has appeared in various magazines throughout North America and been broadcast on CBC Radio.

Arthur was born in Moose Jaw, raised on a ranch in the Cypress Hills of Saskatchewan, and further educated at the University of Saskatchewan (B.A. Honours English). He writes full time from his home in Saskatoon and spends a good portion of his year giving readings and presentations at schools across the country. Arthur may be visited virtually at http://www.arthurslade.com or e-mailed at art@arthurslade.com.

In the same collection

Ven Begamudré, *Isaac Brock: Larger Than Life.*
Lynne Bowen, *Robert Dunsmuir: Laird of the Mines.*
Kate Braid, *Emily Carr: Rebel Artist.*
William Chalmers, *George Mercer Dawson: Geologist, Scientist, Explorer.*
Stephen Eaton Hume, *Frederick Banting: Hero, Healer, Artist.*
Betty Keller, *Pauline Johnson: First Aboriginal Voice of Canada.*
Dave Margoshes, *Tommy Douglas: Building the New Society.*
Raymond Plante, *Jacques Plante: Behind the Mask.*
John Wilson, *John Franklin: Traveller on Undiscovered Seas.*
John Wilson, *Norman Bethune: A Life of Passionate Conviction.*
Rachel Wyatt, *Agnes Macphail: Champion of the Underdog.*

John Diefenbaker

Canadian Cataloguing in Publication Data

Slade, Arthur G. (Arthur Gregory)

    John Diefenbaker: an appointment with destiny

    (The Quest Library ; 9).
    Includes bibliographical references and index.

    ISBN 0-9688166-0-6

    1. Diefenbaker, John G., 1895-1979. 2. Canada – Politics and government – 1957-1963. 3. Prime ministers – Canada – Biography. I. Title. II. Series: Quest library; 9.

FC616.D53S48 2001   971.064'2'092   C2001-940386-0
F1034.3.D.53S48 2001

Legal Deposit: Second quarter 2001
National Library of Canada
Bibliothèque nationale du Québec

XYZ Publishing acknowledges the support of The Quest Library project by the Canadian Studies Program and the Book Publishing Industry Development Program (BPIDP) of the Department of Canadian Heritage. The opinions expressed do not necessarily reflect the views of the Government of Canada.

The publishers further acknowledge the financial support our publishing program receives from The Canada Council for the Arts, the ministère de la Culture et des Communications du Québec, and the Société de développement des entreprises culturelles.

Chronology and Index: Lynne Bowen
Layout: Édiscript enr.
Cover design: Zirval Design
Cover illustration: Francine Auger
John Diefenbaker's signature: National Archives of Canada/PA-130070
Photo research: Arthur Slade & Rhonda Bailey

Printed and bound in Canada

XYZ Publishing   Distributed by:
1781 Saint Hubert Street   General Distribution Services
Montreal, Quebec H2L 3Z1   325 Humber College Boulevard
Tel: (514) 525-2170   Toronto, Ontario M9W 7C3
Fax: (514) 525-7537   Tel: (416) 213-1919
E-mail: xyzed@mlink.net   Fax: (416) 213-1917
Web site: www.xyzedit.com   E-mail: cservice@genpub.com

DIEFENBAKER

John

AN APPOINTMENT WITH DESTINY

XYZ
Publishing

Contents

John George Diefenbaker as a child, seated, with his brother Elmer at his side. "Someday I am going to be prime minister."

1

"I'm going to be prime minister!"

The Métis man with the fierce, determined eyes was known to have killed at least a dozen men during the Riel Rebellion of 1885. He sat in the Diefenbaker house, a gun at his side. He was sixty-eight years old, but his hair was dark black. It had been parted to hide the scar from a bullet that had grazed him during the rebellion.

His name was Gabriel Dumont.

Young John Diefenbaker, just eight years old, couldn't stop staring at the stranger. John's heart raced. He knew this guerrilla fighter had guided the Métis to victory during the Battle of Duck Lake, less than twenty years ago. That battle had been fought only a few kilometres from the Diefenbaker home, staining the snow red with blood. Prime Minister John A. Macdonald ordered General Middleton to take the Canadian army by train to the territories and end the fighting. Over five thousand soldiers descended on Batoche, with Gatling guns and cannons blazing. The Canadian army won, Dumont fled to the United States, and Louis Riel, the rebel leader, was hanged. Fifteen months later the government issued a general amnesty to all the rebels, hoping to quell feelings of anger in Quebec over Riel's death.

Young John couldn't believe Dumont was here – right in their house. He had stopped by for a visit while hunting game. Everything about the man was intimidating; his size, his demeanor, his dark, serious eyes. He was part of history. John didn't know if he trusted Dumont, but he did admire him.

Dumont would be the first of many famous men whom John Diefenbaker would meet in his lifetime. In the following years, Diefenbaker grew to understand why the Riel Rebellion had been fought and recognized the problems faced by the First Nations people, the Métis, and the less fortunate in Canada. But on the day Gabriel Dumont had dropped by their home on the prairie, John was still a child. A little frightened, a little worried, but sitting on the edge of his chair ready to pick up any new revelations about Canada's history.

∞

William Thomas Diefenbaker, John's father, was born in Ontario and never intended to move west. He was a short man, with a friendly face and well-trimmed mustache and the wide-eyed look of a dreamer. He also loved books and trained in Ottawa to be a teacher. His second love was politics: he spent his spare time in the House of Commons gallery watching the Canadian government in action. John A. Macdonald, Canada's first prime minister, was serving his last year in office. An election was brewing and William heard many grand speeches. "The House of Commons lived for him," John Diefenbaker later explained, "and it lived for me when I heard him recount the events he had witnessed and stories of the parliamentary personalities he had seen."

William began his life as a teacher and, oddly enough, one of his students was a boy named Mackenzie King, who would one day become prime minister. In 1894 William Diefenbaker married Mary Bannerman, a strong-willed, straight-backed woman of Scottish descent who was a devout Baptist.

On the 18th of September, 1895, their first son was born: John George Diefenbaker. He had clear blue eyes and soon grew an unruly mop of blonde hair (it would darken as he aged). He was a lad stuffed full of questions, eager to know everything. He could be a precocious little devil too. He enjoyed watching aristocrats from Toronto, out for a Sunday drive, pass by his home town in their newfangled electric cars. Whenever one of the untrustworthy vehicles broke down, leaving the rich men and women stuck kilometres from home in their best clothes, John would dash up and taunt them with questions like, "Do you think it will *ever* start again?" This led to the men yelling and stamping their feet while John ran giggling away.

Lucky for John he was not alone in his youthful adventures. His brother, Elmer, was born in 1897. Elmer was an outgoing and happy-go-lucky child, the perfect sidekick. Diefenbaker later wrote, "Our relationship over the years approached that often described but seldom encountered ideal." In other words, they were brothers and friends.

But John had a serious side as a child too. He became acquainted with black boys who were often badly treated by others. Even at this early age John said, "The idea of the poor being treated differently, the working man being looked down upon as a digit, filled me with revulsion."

John's idyllic childhood was interrupted by bad news: TB. In the spring of 1903 William was diagnosed with Galloping Consumption, a type of tuberculosis that affected both lungs. He was advised to seek the healthy benefits of the dry prairie climate. William immediately secured a position in what was then part of the North-West Territories, but is today known as Saskatchewan.

When the relatives found out the Diefenbakers were leaving Ontario to live in the sticks, Mary's brother said, "What's the matter with you? Going to that awful country where there's nothing but bears and Indians – they'll kill you!" This was exactly the wrong thing to say. Mary Diefenbaker, never one to back down once a decision was made, announced they were going to go no matter what.

The Canadian prairie was still a land of homesteads and opportunities, and the trains were packed with immigrants of all nationalities hoping to get a piece of prairie farmland and make a life for themselves. The Diefenbakers could only afford colonist class, with no sleeping accommodations and no dining car. Mary had prepared for this by sending blankets and food early to the train with William, but unfortunately a railway official gave William bad directions and he stored the supplies on the wrong train. The Diefenbakers got by with the help of fellow passengers who shared their food and blankets. At night, the boys slept tied to a wooden shelf on the wall so they wouldn't fall out.

The cramped quarters and constant jostling got on William's nerves. Part way to the Prairies, he announced they were returning to Ontario.

Mary narrowed her eyes. "We started out and we're going on!" she said.

William insisted he'd go back on his own if he had to.

"If you do, the rest of us will carry on and you'll come out sooner or later."

William finally agreed she was right. This wouldn't be the last argument he lost to Mary. "Well, you know," he would often say, "Mary is always right. Sometimes I don't think so at the time, but it always turns out to be the proper course to take."

That course took them out of the trees and rocky land of the Canadian Shield and into the level prairie landscape. They went through Winnipeg and Regina, then headed northwest to Saskatoon (which only had a population of five hundred at the time) and finally stepped off the train in the town of Rosthern. After a two-night rest in the Queen's Hotel, the Diefenbakers loaded their possessions into a wagon and bumped across the old prairie trails, steering around coulees lined with trees and fields of golden wheat. Finally, the Diefenbakers arrived at their destination: Tiefengrund school.

The Diefenbakers were now thousands of kilometres from their relatives in Eastern Canada. They didn't know a soul, but that changed quickly because their living quarters were attached to the schoolhouse, which was also a community meeting place. Gabriel Dumont would drop in or sometimes members of the North West Mounted Police stopped, including the very officers who'd fought against Dumont. In fact, Sergeant Pook, a regular visitor who liked Mary Diefenbaker's cooking, told tales of how enemy bullets twice tore through his clothing during the rebellion without hitting him. These stories stuck with John his whole life and gave him a pride in the Mounted Police that never faded. People from the reserve would stop by for tea, and their tales of Indian lore and history also had a deep effect on young John.

∞

His father's health stayed strong. William would often take John hunting and fishing, a recreation that John would enthusiastically pursue for the rest of his life. John also discovered a love for reading that equaled his father's. There were always books in their home to be read by the light of a coal-oil lamp: Shakespeare, *Gibbon's Decline and Fall of the Roman Empire* and a broken set of *Ridpath's History of the World*.

They celebrated the creation of the province of Saskatchewan on September 1, 1905. John's father, who organized the celebration in Hague, bought a couple of dozen Union Jacks and put them up all across town. Then the villagers gathered in the schoolhouse to sing "The Maple Leaf Forever" and "God Save the King."

One day, when he was nine years old, John was reading about Prime Minister Laurier. The book reminded John that he had an important announcement. Something that had been building inside his head for a long time. It was a declaration of who he wanted to be. Or was it his destiny? he wondered. Finally he looked up at his mother and said, "Someday I am going to be prime minister." His mother, always serious, was silent for a long time. She hadn't laughed, and he thought this was a good sign. She didn't think he was making up a story. She told him it would be very difficult since he lived so far out on the Prairies, but she finished by saying, "If you work hard enough, there's no reason why you shouldn't." John never forgot these words.

∽

He was shy, though, and averse to public speaking. He attended meetings at the Farmers' Institute with his father. These were information sessions about current problems like the difficulties in selling wheat on the market and how individual farmers weren't able to stand up in court against farm machinery companies with faulty equipment.

During one of these meetings, John, now thirteen years old, became so upset about the way homesteaders were treated he launched himself to his feet and blustered, "This thing is wrong. Some day I'm going to do my part to put an end to this."

The thirty or so people present applauded loudly. "I was so frightened," he later wrote, "that I could hardly get out the words."

He would soon overcome his stage fright.

∞

Diefenbaker was a long way from reaching his goal of becoming prime minister of Canada. His family moved several times, and in 1910 came to Saskatoon so that John and Elmer would get a good education. Saskatoon had experienced a boom – over ten thousand people were now living in this frontier city by the river. John found a job as a newspaper boy and was soon selling the Saskatoon *Phoenix*, the Winnipeg *Tribune*, and the Calgary *Eye-Opener*. During this work, he had an encounter that would stay with him the rest of his life.

∞

John was in a hurry. The rising sun painted the train station red. He rushed down to the unloading platform and gathered up his papers. He had to hand sell them, then get to school. He never had time to chit-chat with the other paper-boys or anyone else. He'd never get ahead that way.

Then a door to a private railway car opened. John paused to stare. Someone rich had to be inside, maybe a bigwig with the railway. A man dressed in a suit stepped out, breathed deeply of the prairie air. His thick hair was white as rabbit's fur. He certainly looked important and dignified.

Then the man turned. John recognized his face. It was the prime minister of Canada, Sir Wilfrid Laurier. He was in town to lay the first cornerstone for the University of Saskatchewan. *I bet I can sell a paper to him*, John thought. He strode up to the prime minister.

Laurier smiled. He handed John twenty-five cents for a five-cent paper. John felt flushed with success. *I'll ask him a question about Canada*, John decided. Laurier replied kindly and the two chatted casually for a few minutes about John's interest in politics, and the tasks of being prime minister. But the paper-boy clock in the back of John's mind was still ticking. He *had* to sell his papers. "Sorry, Prime Minister," he announced, "I can't waste any more time on you, I've got work to do." And he hurried on to sell the rest of his newspapers.

∽

This brief meeting became a turning point in John's life: "Sir Wilfrid inspired me with the idea that each of us, no matter who he is or what his upbringing, or however humble his parentage and home, can rise to any position in this country, provided we dedicate ourselves."

And so John set to dedicating himself. How do you become a politician? How do you become leader of the land? He read biographies and soon recognized there were two things he had to master to achieve his goal of getting into politics: public speaking and the law.

He was especially drawn to the law because he had read the biography of Abraham Lincoln, who had started as a small town lawyer and had risen to become the president of the United States. It seemed the obvious path to take.

John graduated from Saskatoon Collegiate in June of 1912. By September he was in his first year at the University of Saskatchewan, studying history, political science, and economics. He got a taste of politics by taking part in the university's mock parliament and the first provincial Boys Parliament in Regina. In his second year he became the leader of the Conservative party in mock parliament and leader of the Opposition in the Boy's Parliament.

By his third year the graduation issue of *The Sheaf* predicted that in forty years, in 1955, Diefenbaker would be the leader of the Opposition in the Canadian House of Commons. They were only off by one year.

But soon, John felt the call of war. Britain and the Commonwealth, including Canada, were locked in a deadly struggle against Germany in the fields of France. World War One had been underway for two years and John believed it was the duty of every able-bodied citizen to sign up.

In March of 1916 he enlisted. By May he received his commission as Lieutenant in the Infantry of the Active Militia, and on September 23rd, he boarded the SS *Lapland* and sailed for England.

2

Lawyer for the Defence

"Do you realize that sixty-five per cent of you will be pushing up daisies within three months?"

Diefenbaker and his fellow officers were bunked down on a cold concrete floor at Napier Barracks in Shorncliffe, England. The officer who had just called out had already been wounded at the front and had recovered enough to be sent back again. He wanted to let the boys know exactly what they were in for. Artillery echoing across the Channel added doom to his words. The officer shouted his question every time the group tried to sleep.

It was a harsh welcome for Diefenbaker and a sign of what was to come for him and his friends. They

Young lawyer in Wakaw, September 1919.
Diefenbaker would win his first trial and become
one of Saskatchewan's most prosperous lawyers.

continued training in England while they waited to be sent to the front. Diefenbaker worked hard at the physically exhausting labour of digging trenches – perhaps too hard – for within a month he reported spitting up blood and shortness of breath. He was diagnosed with "disordered action of the heart" and within a short time had been judged unable to serve. He returned to Canada. Like his father, John had a weak constitution, but he still wanted to do his part for "King and Country." He tried to enroll in the Royal Flying Corps but was turned down. Sadly, several of his friends who travelled overseas never returned.

His brief military career over, John could now pursue his goal of becoming a lawyer. The University of Saskatchewan, like other Canadian universities, gave credit for war service, so Diefenbaker was able to graduate. In the spring of 1919 he wrote and passed his finals and received his law degree.

"Gentlemen of the Jury, have you reached your verdict?" The Clerk of the Court asked.

"We have."

"How say you? Is the prisoner guilty or not guilty?"

"Not guilty."

With those two words in the fall of 1919 the career of John Diefenbaker, lawyer for the defence, was launched. It was his first victory, and news that the boy with the piercing blue eyes was a dynamite lawyer spread like wildfire through Wakaw and the surrounding area.

Diefenbaker had defended John Chernyski, a farmer who had stepped out of his house at twilight, seen his dogs wrestling with what looked like a fox or a coyote and had let go with both barrels of his shotgun. The animal yelped and then called out, "help!"

The victim was actually a neighbor boy who'd been crossing the field on his bike. He was wounded. Chernyski scrambled to take the boy to hospital.

Chernyski ended up in court charged with intent to cause grievous bodily harm. His wife convinced Diefenbaker to defend Chernyski – for a fee of six hundred dollars. Diefenbaker argued that the farmer had made a simple mistake: he'd gone from a brightly lit home to twilight without waiting for his eyes to adjust before pulling the trigger. There was no intention to cause another human being harm. The jury convened and decided John's argument had been compelling enough to render a verdict of "Not guilty." In his memoirs, John wrote that the jury was being kind to him because it was his birthday. If that truly was what motivated their decision then it was perhaps the best birthday present Diefenbaker had in his lifetime.

∞

The small town of Wakaw, Saskatchewan, where Diefenbaker's law office was located, had a population of six hundred. John had chosen the town after examining court records that showed Wakaw was, in his words, "particularly litigious, in court at a moment's notice." What better place for a lawyer to be! It was also close to Saskatoon, which made visiting his parents easy. There was another lawyer in town, but winning the Chernyski case helped John gain a good reputation.

He had sixty-two trials in his first year of practice and won half of them. He would sometimes travel between villages on an old railway handcar, but by the summer of 1920 he paid off a few of his debts, moved into a larger office and bought a Maxwell touring car at a price of $1764.00.

"It was a thing of beauty," John later said, "if not a joy forever." Sadly, tires in those days were not all that dependable. "The only good thing about it was its name... I lost all count of the flat tires. But I loved to tour." The boy who used to taunt the wealthy in their newfangled automobiles now had a car of his own.

It wasn't all about money, touring around, and winning court cases, for John there was a real stake in defending the innocent and the downtrodden: "When I accepted a case where I thought someone's rights were being violated, often the person couldn't pay me, or did so only after many years. From the beginning of my practice, I never charged a Métis or an Indian who came to me for advice. I was distressed by their conditions, the unbelievable poverty and the injustice done them."

He lived frugally and threw himself into his work, though he did take the time to drive to Vancouver in 1921 and Los Angeles in 1923, long trips over unpaved roads, and he also bought a summer cottage at Wakaw Lake, where he could fish and hunt.

∞

Diefenbaker wasn't as lucky in love as he was in court; he remained ill at ease with young women. He blamed this shyness on his childhood: "I am sorry, particularly sorry, that Elmer and I were to grow up without sisters. Given our later isolation on the homestead, our separation from other boys and girls, it became natural to think of women as a species apart, an experience destined to leave a permanent mark on one's attitude toward them." In those days an acquaintance described John this way: "He was tall, slim, quiet, aloof, not aggressive, a very poor mixer." The lawyer who was known for his powerful performance in court was not so powerful on the dance floor.

John became infatuated with Olive Freeman, the young daughter of the minister at First Baptist Church in Saskatoon. He gathered up all his courage and asked her for a date, but she moved with her family to Brandon in 1921 before he could pursue a relationship. Diefenbaker later became engaged to a woman named Beth Newell, but she was diagnosed with tuberculosis and died in 1924.

John himself still suffered from his own physical weaknesses. After several minor hospital stays he travelled to the Mayo Clinic in Rochester, Minnesota and had surgery for a gastric ulcer, which led to some improvement in his health. He didn't stop working though, and he soon felt it was time to perform on a bigger stage: Prince Albert.

∞

Prince Albert in 1924 was a raucous frontier city booming with money, politics, and law cases. Once it had dreamed of being the capital of the North-West Territories, and now it was a gateway to the riches of northern Saskatchewan. The law office door on the second floor of the red brick Bank d'Hochelaga build- ing on Second Avenue read: John G. Diefenbaker Law Office – Walk In. Inside were two used bookcases, a gooseneck lamp, and an oversized desk. Looming behind that desk was John Diefenbaker, now a sea- soned veteran of the daily battles in court.

He took on any case that came his way: bad debts, estates, minor thefts, assault, insurance claims, and slander. Not all as exciting as defending someone against a charge of murder, but he was in a city now. Residents of Prince Albert soon grew accustomed to seeing a confident young lawyer in a three-piece suit striding up and down the streets, or driving his 1927 Chrysler Sedan.

He did make enemies. T.C. Davis, who was a Liberal, the attorney general of the province, and the owner of the Prince Albert *Herald*, didn't much like Diefenbaker, especially because of Diefenbaker's support of the Conservative party. In fact, when Diefenbaker's court cases were written up in the *Herald*, Diefenbaker discovered the reporters wouldn't mention his name; they just called him "a lawyer from Prince Albert." Clients came to him anyway, despite the lack of press.

∞

A slight, pretty young schoolteacher stood on a train platform in Saskatoon. Red hair. A fashionable dress. A light laugh. It was enough to make a young man fall in love.

That's exactly what happened to John. John was introduced to Edna May Brower through his brother. Edna was a "flapper," a term used at the time to describe a woman who was free-willed and unconventional. She wore the latest fashions and loved social events, and though she was engaged to a Langham farmer, she soon only had eyes for John. As one friend explained it, Edna's photograph album, which was filled with pictures of Edna with other men, eventually only had pictures of her and John, swimming, laughing, and picnicking together.

Not everyone saw why these two opposites were attracted to each other. A teaching colleague, Molly Connell, recalled: "His eyes, they just bored right through you. They were like steel; hard eyes. There was never any tenderness or warmth about John Diefenbaker. I felt it then, but one does not say that to a good friend who may be in love with him."

There were others who also didn't understand, but the couple grew closer and closer together.

∞

On a still summer night, John and Edna are alone in the moonlight. They sit with hands entwined. Here is a woman he can trust. In his quietest voice he whispers about how awkward he feels in public and tells her of his wish to become prime minister, because it is "more than a goal; it is my destiny."

Like John's mother so many years before, Edna does not laugh. She looks at this man who is a hawk in court but a wallflower in social situations. She sees the ambition in his eyes. Desire. She knows it will be hard to teach him how to relax in public. To remember people's names. But she is a good teacher. They begin discussing how this goal can be accomplished.

∞

In the spring of 1929 in Walmer Road Baptist Church in Toronto, John George Diefenbaker and Edna May Brower were married. The wedding was in Toronto because that was where Edna's brother's lived.

John suddenly emerged from his shell. At the reception he moved through the crowd with Edna, talking, joking, shaking hands and hugging her. Not a trace of aloofness. Not even an awkward moment. And to top it all off, he even danced with Edna.

That put to rest the gossip that she had chosen a dud.

They returned to Prince Albert and John continued his career. But with the support of his wife, he was a stronger man.

And his legal practice had grown by leaps and bounds. He now employed two lawyers and eight secretaries and had a yearly take-home pay of $4573.00. He was one of Saskatchewan's most prosperous lawyers.

∞

A shotgun blast in the middle of the day. Nick Pasowesty, a successful farmer, was murdered on his own land. No one knew who pulled the trigger, but an RCMP investigation found the family weapon that fired the shell and discovered that Pasowesty was highly disliked by his neighbor and had a rather rocky relationship with his third wife, Annie. The Mounties dug deeper and quickly focused on the youngest son, John, a spendthrift seventeen-year-old who had apparently bragged about shooting his dad.

After a brief interrogation, the boy confessed to the crime. A week later he changed his tune, saying his mother had pulled the trigger. "She told me that I should say that I have killed my old man because I might get out of it somehow because she would get some lawyers for me."

That lawyer turned out to be John Diefenbaker and this was his first murder case. He faced an uphill climb – the trial judge was Mr. Justice George E. Taylor, who had been intimidating defence lawyers for over forty years. He preferred prosecution to leniency and Diefenbaker had butted heads with him a number of times in the past.

John first questioned Annie on the stand, but several lines of inquiry were shot down by the judge. Next Diefenbaker tried to convince the judge that the boy's first confession was inadmissible because the boy was under stress and had been arrested without being allowed to speak to his family. The judge cut Diefenbaker off and explained that the confession would stand: "I must say that I feel so convinced that I could not hope that any further consideration of the matter would alter the conclusion at which I have arrived."

Diefenbaker began to sweat. He had to put doubt in the jury's mind by implicating the boy's mother. Unfortunately Diefenbaker had made a serious mistake, he hadn't subpoenaed the RCMP officer who wrote down the boy's second confession. Diefenbaker had believed the prosecution would call the officer. Too late, Diefenbaker asked to call his witness up. The judge disallowed the request and rebuked Diefenbaker in front of the whole courtroom. "If you want evidence," the judge lectured, "it is your duty to get it yourself. Proceed please."

Diefenbaker had only one choice left. He put the boy in the witness box. The prosecution carefully and politely tore holes in the boy's suggestion that his mother was the killer. By the time the prosecution was finished, the boy looked like a cunning murderer.

"Annie Pasowesty," Diefenbaker said in his closing arguments, "committed this crime. A schemer, a plotter, she contrived an arrangement where she could kill her husband and throw suspicion upon her son. And worse. Then she induced this boy to confess to the crime, to take that responsibility upon himself and steer all suspicion away from her." He hoped his words would be enough to put doubt in the minds of the jury.

The prosecution continued to insist the boy could not be believed. The judge echoed that conclusion.

Five hours later the jury returned with a verdict of guilty and the judge sentenced John Pasowesty to be hanged at Prince Albert jail on February 21, 1930.

It was a loss, but Diefenbaker, who disliked capital punishment, had one final ace to play. He had a psychiatrist examine the boy. The conclusion: John Pasowesty had a mental age of eight or nine years.

With this new information John petitioned the federal cabinet for clemency, and the boy's sentence was commuted to life imprisonment.

"I knew I wouldn't die," John Pasowesty sobbed as he clutched the telegram from Ottawa. "I don't know about spending the rest of my life in jail, but I think I'll like it better than hanging."

For Diefenbaker, it was almost a victory.

The Pasowesty trial was immediately followed by Diefenbaker's second murder case, which he took on without a fee. His client, a Polish immigrant named Alex Wysochan, was involved in a love triangle that ended with the death of Antena Kropa, and her husband was the only witness. Stanley Kropa's version was that Alex Wysochan, his wife's lover, had broken into the Kropa house while drunk and threatened to shoot him. Stanley leapt out a window then heard four shots and his wife's anguished cry. The police arrived to find Antena fatally wounded, and her lover lying drunk beside her.

Wysochan, who spoke only through a Polish interpreter, had a different version of events. He said that Stanley had found him drinking at the Windsor Hotel and invited him home, then started a fight and pulled out a gun. Antena got between them, four shots rang out, and Antena crumpled to the ground. Wysochan collapsed in a drunken stupor.

Diefenbaker, who was suffering from his gastric ulcer and had been bedridden for parts of the trial, tried to convince the jury that Wysochan's story was true. At first he advised his client to stay off the witness stand and say he didn't remember anything of the night. That way the charges might be lowered to manslaughter and Wysochan would only have to spend ten years in jail. "I'm innocent, why should I?" Wysochan replied. He went to the stand. The jury, all men of British background, took an immediate dislike to this European immigrant who drank and had committed adultery.

"Admittedly, Alex Wysochan dishonoured the Kropa home," Diefenbaker said in his closing arguments, "Admittedly, he was immoral in his relations with Antena Kropa. But he is not charged with these things. He is here today charged with the killing of Antena Kropa, the woman he loved and had no reason to kill."

The prosecuting lawyer didn't take a rational, calm approach to his closing arguments. Instead, he called Alex "this little rat," "this reptile," and "the dirty little coward."

The jury convened for five hours, broke for the night, and in the morning returned with a guilty verdict. Wysochan was sentenced to the gallows and the judge immediately called up the next case. Diefenbaker just happened to represent the next defendant, too. He had a brutally hard day.

Diefenbaker filed an appeal for Wysochan's verdict, but no reprieve was granted and Alex Wysochan was hanged in Prince Albert on June 20, 1930.

"A few months after the trial it was established that he was innocent," Diefenbaker said in his memoirs. For him, to have a client hung was the ultimate failure. "My profound respect for human life is based on religious conviction. I do not believe in capital punishment."

From 1930 to 1936 Diefenbaker fought four more murder cases. A woman accused of smothering her newborn child was found not guilty. A grand success. Diefenbaker was becoming a dramatic genius. He had learned how to use his penetrating eyes and to control his voice so the jury would hang on every word. Many a witness feared to face John in court.

Even the RCMP could be intimidated by Diefenbaker. "I was anything but the serene and confident Mountie I appeared to be," admitted Constable Arthur Cookson, "It was his eyes most of all."

Cookson was the investigating detective in the trial of Steve Bohun, a nineteen-year-old accused of shooting and robbing a postmaster. Diefenbaker defended Bohun, using every technique he had mastered. He wanted to prove that the Mounties had forced Bohun to confess. "Do you understand the nature of an oath?" he boomed, starting his cross-examination of Cookson. The constable was an impressive man decked out in his RCMP dress uniform of redcoat, breeches and high boots, but he soon felt flustered as Diefenbaker paced the floor or stood facing the spectators, firing questions over his shoulder for over an hour and a half. "You showed him the blood stains still upon the floor, the blood of the dead Peter Pommereul, didn't you?" Diefenbaker accused. "And then, Constable Cookson, then you tried to force this young boy to put his hands upon those blood stains. What do you say to that?" Diefenbaker suddenly turned and thrust out a long accusatory finger. It was a move he would become famous for in the House of Commons.

"I did no such thing," Cookson replied, rising to his feet. But a seed of doubt had been planted in the jury's mind.

Diefenbaker was at his dramatic best but the jury found Bohun guilty, though they did ask for mercy because of his lack of intelligence. The judge sentenced him to hang.

On March 9, 1934, John walked out to his front porch. From there he had a view of the Prince Albert prison. A black flag was raised slowly up the flagpole, signalling Steve Bohun's death. Diefenbaker wept, jaws clenched, tears staining his cheeks. "Poor devil," he whispered, "poor, poor devil."

In Diefenbaker's next case, the violent murder of a farmer near Leask, the prosecution didn't have enough evidence to continue the trial, so Diefenbaker won by default. Next came a front-page murder trial. Two trappers had gotten drunk, and in an argument over their take, one had shot the other dead. Diefenbaker was able to get the charge lowered to manslaughter because the culprit had been drinking.

John Diefenbaker had made a name for himself and had become the lawyer he wanted to be.

He had one more goal to achieve.

A shot of Edna in the 1930s,
stylish as always.

A 1933 ad urging the public
to meet Diefenbaker.

3

Running for Election

In 1911, when John Diefenbaker was fifteen years old, Liberal Prime Minister Wilfrid Laurier called an election. Laurier had been running Canada like a well-oiled machine since 1896. He had created the provinces of Saskatchewan and Alberta. He had opened the floodgates to immigrants and the population of the dominion had grown from four million to seven million. He was the first and perhaps the greatest French Canadian leader, able to balance Quebec interests with the interests and the demands of the rest of Canada. He was known as the "Knight of the White Plume," and he predicted bravely that the twentieth century belonged to Canada. Laurier wanted another term, so he called the election and ran on the platform of reciprocity – freer trade with the United States.

It was a big mistake. The Conservatives, led by Robert Borden, unfurled their Red Ensigns and waved them like mad, singing "Yankee Doodle Laurier." They believed open trade with the U.S. would lead to stronger economic and political union with the Americans and eventually Canada's sovereignty would be diminished. After all, Canada was only forty-four years old and still had important ties to Britain. And then "Champ" Clark, the Speaker of the U.S. House of Representatives, declared his support for reciprocity because he hoped, "to see the day when the American flag will float over every square foot of the British North American Colonies clear to the North Pole." This didn't help Laurier's cause one iota. His campaign was dealt another blow when Clark announced, "We are preparing to annex Canada." The flag-waving and the shouting of the Conservatives grew to near pandemonium. Laurier was voted out of office *tout de suite*.

Young Diefenbaker watched this firestorm of emotion and politics with wide-open eyes. "The election had a profound influence on me, and perhaps more than anything else made me a Conservative," Diefenbaker wrote many years later. "I attended all the meetings in Saskatoon. The Tories had a marvellous campaign. They didn't have any arguments but they raised the flag and we'd sing… 'We're soldiers of the King.' The result was a tremendous revelation of Canadian determination to be Canadian. This impressed me greatly." The impression would last a lifetime.

John had done exceedingly well in the mock parliaments during his university years, but the first real test of his speaking skill came when he was elected to city council in Wakaw, by a slim margin of twelve votes.

People began to notice this brash upstart, and the Liberal party tried to enlist John in 1921. He declined. They were flabbergasted. Who in their right mind wouldn't want to join the Liberal party? So one day when John was out of town the Wakaw Liberal Association elected him secretary, sneaked into his office, and left their minute books and pamphlets on his desk. When he got back and discovered this, he immediately marched to the Liberal president and gave the books back.

On June 19, 1925, Diefenbaker let the world know he was a Conservative. Well, actually he addressed a small group of Conservatives at an organizing meeting in a tiny room in Prince Albert, but it felt like he was telling the whole world. It was his first official act as a Conservative. His feet were wet, so he dived in and two months later was declared the party's federal candidate by acclamation.

He might as well have been invisible. The Liberals were already in power both federally and provincially, and the Conservatives were at the bottom of the political heap, with no real hope of a victory in Saskatchewan.

The election was called for October 29, 1925. Diefenbaker squared off against Charles Macdonald, the Liberal candidate. The war of words was fast and furious, and at one point John was described by his opponents as a "Hun." This was an attempt to identify

Diefenbaker with the German forces who had been the enemy in the First World War. "Matters were made little better when I was simply called a German," John later recalled, "I was not a German, not a German-Canadian, but a Canadian." Diefenbaker, as he would repeat throughout his lifetime, was always a Canadian first. During a speech at the Orpheum Theatre in Prince Albert he attacked his opponents by saying: "Am I German? My great-grandfather left Germany to seek liberty. My grandfather and my father were born in Canada. It is true, however, that my grandmother and my grandfather on my mother's side spoke no English: being Scottish, they spoke Gaelic. If there is no hope for me to be Canadian, then who is there hope for?"

It was a rousing reply, though he had slightly stretched the truth: his Diefenbaker grandfather was born in Germany and his Bannerman grandparents spoke English. The point was still the same.

But just as Diefenbaker was fighting off his opponents' claims, he was sideswiped by the leader of his own party. Arthur Meighen was a hard-minded, steely-eyed man who had briefly been prime minister (he succeeded Robert Borden in 1920 and was voted out of office in 1921). Meighen declared he would alter the Crow's Nest Pass freight rate, which was subsidized to keep the grain flowing to the West Coast cheaply. Meighen also opposed the completion of a Hudson Bay railway, which would give farmers in Saskatchewan another outlet for their grain.

Diefenbaker publicly disagreed with his own leader, and it didn't win him any points with his party.

"My position was difficult," Diefenbaker later wrote. "It need not have been. But I chose to speak for myself." This wouldn't be the last time he would follow his own path instead of toeing the party line.

He campaigned tirelessly through every small town and hall in his constituency, but there was no hope. Even though the Conservatives won the most seats in Parliament, they did not get a clear majority and Mackenzie King remained prime minister. The news was even worse for Diefenbaker: not one Conservative was elected in Saskatchewan.

But party supporters who witnessed his valiant battle wouldn't forget the name of John G. Diefenbaker anytime soon. Diefenbaker was soon invited to speak at other conventions, always making an impression. Bruce Hutchinson, a reporter covering a convention of the British Columbia Conservative party, wrote: "From this frail, wraith-like person, so deceptive in his look of physical infirmity, a voice of vehement power and rude health blared like a trombone." If Diefenbaker was a trombone, the song he was playing was one of frustration. He would play quite a few sad tunes before he could blast away in the House of Commons.

Almost a year later, Mackenzie King was hit with a scandal over corruption in the customs department. He asked for the dissolution of Parliament, but the Governor General refused and Conservative leader Arthur Meighen became the next prime minister. He was promptly defeated and the next day the headlines announced a new election.

If the fight was hard last time for Diefenbaker, this time he was up against the political heavyweight champion of Canada. William Lyon Mackenzie King himself ran in Diefenbaker's riding because in the previous election King had lost in his home riding. King, who had been groomed by Laurier, was a wily opponent well versed in political sparring. Stocky and intelligent, he had been prime minister since 1921, except for Meighen's brief interlude.

Diefenbaker geared himself up for another battle but was blindsided once again by his own party. Arthur Meighen was completely opposed to the Liberals' old age pension plan, which was something voters wanted. Diefenbaker thought the pension was just a matter of plain, honest decency. Meighen also continued spouting out his views on the Crow's Nest Pass rates and the Hudson Bay Railway.

By constant touring, Diefenbaker overcame these problems. He even gained ground on the prime minister. Could the impossible happen? Could Diefenbaker actually defeat Mackenzie King?

Chances for such an upset were dashed when the *Toronto Telegram* reported that a top Conservative in the east, R.J. Manion, claimed that 99 per cent of Prince Albert voters were immigrants with hard-to-pronounce names: "Mackenzie King has gone to Prince Albert, has left North York. He doesn't like the smell of native-born Canadians. He prefers the stench of garlic-stinking continentals, Eskimos, bohunks, and Indians."

His statement hit the papers across the country. For Diefenbaker, who had one of those hard-to-pronounce last names, this was a terrible blow. Liberal pamphlets flooded Prince Albert saying: "Citizens of Prince Albert: Mark your ballot for Mackenzie King and reject this insult!" The final tally of votes in Prince Albert was Mackenzie King 4,838, Diefenbaker 3,933. The Liberals won a majority of seats, and only one Conservative was returned to power in the western provinces – R.B. Bennett, a rich tycoon. Meighen lost his seat.

∞

On a cool October night in 1928 a thin stranger slinks into the rear of a hall in Hawarden, Saskatchewan and seats himself in a dimly lit corner. The place is packed with Liberals. They're edgy because in two days a provincial by-election vote will be held in Arm River constituency, and it has been a drop-kick, drag-'em-out battle – a sign that the upcoming provincial election will be even tougher. The Conservatives are pressing the Liberals to explain their patronage practices and the presence of Catholic nuns and teachings in public schools.

This meeting is intended to bring the Liberal ranks together. Premier Jimmy Gardiner and his Minister of Agriculture, C.M. Hamilton, are there to speak. The crowd of three hundred waits in anticipation.

Mr. Hamilton walks to the front of the stage. He extols the virtue of his government's record, but the stranger interrupts him part way through the speech, then again a few minutes later. And again and again.

This is too much for Premier Gardiner, a relentless Liberal, who had served as a member of the legislative assembly in Saskatchewan since 1914. He gathers up all his political outrage and demands, "Who is this person? It takes us little time in Liberal meetings to put an end to characters like you. It's easy to sit down there and ask questions you've been sent to ask, and paid for. Well, I'm going to give you the opportunity to let this audience see and hear you. I'm going to give you the platform for twenty minutes." He smiles.

The stranger stands and Gardiner's smile slips from his face. He squints his eyes as a familiar tall, thin, wraith-like man steps into the light. It is John Diefenbaker.

"The offer doesn't apply to you," Gardiner says quickly. "What are you doing here anyway? I wouldn't let you speak on my platform for anything."

"But you asked me," Diefenbaker replies, striding along until he reaches the foot of the platform. Gardiner continues to protest but Diefenbaker lectures him, saying, "Fairness is essential in every walk of life. You challenged me, and I'm here."

The audience begins to murmur, then to yell, "Let him speak."

Gardiner steps back. "I want to be fair. I'll give you ten minutes."

"No," someone shouts out, "Give him the twenty minutes you promised."

Gardiner sits down and Diefenbaker takes the stage.

"I have some questions in connection with education," he says, then he pauses. "As it appears to be the custom for speakers in this campaign to indicate their religious beliefs, I hereby state that I am a Baptist and I am not a member of the Ku Klux Klan." That declaration out of the way he asks question after question, each embarrassing to the premier and his government. Why are nuns teaching in a public school? When is the Liberal patronage going to stop? Diefenbaker finishes his barrage within ten minutes and returns to his seat.

Somewhat flustered, Gardiner takes the stage again. It's 10:30 p.m. and as he begins his speech, his spine straightens, his voice shakes the rafters, and word after compelling word is launched at the crowd. But he ignores Diefenbaker's questions.

The crowd interrupts, asking him to answer the charges.

"You wait," Gardiner promises. He continues talking and talking and finally, he stops, looks at his watch and announces, "It's midnight. I never discuss politics on Sunday. I believe we should keep Sunday a holy day."

And that was that. On polling day in Arm River, 91 per cent of the population turned out, an extraordinary number for a by-election. The Liberals held onto the seat, but only by fifty-nine votes.

More importantly, this one feisty performance by Diefenbaker caught the attention of a number of people high up in the Conservative party, both federally and provincially. "Out of that meeting at Hawarden," Diefenbaker explained, "stemmed my invitation to contest the federal seat of Long Lake in the 1930 election, my bid for a provincial seat in Arm River in 1938, and finally, my nomination and election to the House of Commons in Lake Centre in 1940."

It was indeed a good night's work.

∞

A provincial election was called for June 6, 1929 and Diefenbaker decided to switch from federal to provincial politics. The Liberals had been ruling Saskatchewan since 1905, but there were holes in the Liberal armour now. People resented the patronage practices. The province was ripe for a Conservative win.

Diefenbaker squared off against his old foe T.C. Davis, who was the owner of the Prince Albert newspaper and the attorney general. Diefenbaker was promised the attorney generalship himself if the Conservatives were victorious.

The mudslinging began at once. The Liberals accused Diefenbaker of working hand in hand with the Ku Klux Klan, a group that was anti-Catholic, anti-Jewish, and against non-English and immigrants of colour. The Klan also hated the Liberal party. Diefenbaker explained that "everyone who opposed Gardiner, his policies, and the viciousness of his machine was tarred with the dirty brush of Klan fanaticism."

The Conservative party won the election, ending twenty-four years in power by the Liberals. Diefenbaker wasn't able to join the celebrations: he lost his riding to Davis by several hundred votes.

John didn't stick around to lick his wounds. Instead, he retreated to Toronto and married Edna.

∞

In 1930 Diefenbaker and Edna were in Toronto for a holiday, so John could relax. His health wasn't getting any better; in fact, he was still suffering from internal bleeding and stomach pains. The stress of his political life and his numerous trials had taken their toll. It was time to rest.

Then a telegram from the Conservative association arrived. John read it carefully, his hands shaking. They wanted him to accept the nomination for the federal riding of Long Lake, a riding that was supposed to be an easy win.

He talked to Edna. He felt the tiredness in his bones. The aching in his stomach. John, who had dreamed of this all his life, was forced to say no. He was too sick. Too tired. He watched sadly from the sidelines as another man won the seat and went to Ottawa.

The country, and particularly the Prairies, was changing for the worse. The stock market had crashed in 1929. The price of wheat, a major Saskatchewan export, began to drop, and the onset of drought made the amount of wheat available for sale even smaller. Next came mass unemployment and a general disenchantment with politicians. This was a tough time to be a government.

By 1933 Diefenbaker began once again to dabble in politics. He was elected as the vice-president of the provincial Conservative party. Later that same year he ran for mayor of Prince Albert and lost by forty-eight votes.

A provincial election was held on June 19, 1934. Diefenbaker didn't run, but he worked desperately behind the scenes. The Conservatives, squeezed by the Liberals on one side and the new Farmer-Labour party on the other, failed to win a single seat.

The western world was in the throes of major political change. Across the ocean the Nazi party unfurled its swastikas in Germany. The Depression continued sending dust cloud after dust cloud into the Prairies. And thousands of unemployed men of all ages now hitched rides on the train to look for work.

In May of 1935 the "On-to-Ottawa" journey was begun from the West Coast. At first there were just a thousand unemployed men packing the freight cars. Then two thousand. Three thousand. The movement gathered steam and support every time the train stopped at a railway station. In Regina the RCMP halted the gathering, and after negotiations and a violent clash that ended with the death of a policeman, the marchers were dispersed. The whole episode made the federal Conservatives, under the leadership of Bennett, look bad.

Parliament was dissolved a few months later. Diefenbaker declined the nomination in Prince Albert saying, "I think this is a time for us to have a farmer as a candidate." A farmer was chosen and Diefenbaker, now the president of the provincial Conservative party, did all he could to help the cause. But it was a mishmash of an election: the Co-operative Commonwealth Federation (CCF) was rising up in the West; Social Credit, an Alberta-based party, was now nominating federally; the brand new Reconstruction party, an offshoot of the Conservatives, appeared; and the Liberals still had their political machine in high gear.

On October 14th it was a landslide for the Liberals, and after all the other parties took a piece of the pie the Conservatives were left with only forty seats.

Diefenbaker continued to wait on the sidelines. He went on a holiday to France, where he visited the Canadian war memorial in memory of the valiant battle of Vimy Ridge. Then he took a trip to Berlin to the Olympic games. "I saw Hitler, Goering, Goebbels, and Dr. Funk. They were within thirty or forty feet of me. I saw at first hand the curse of militarism renewed in the German people. When I returned home to Prince Albert I made a speech expressing the certainty that war was coming."

But war wasn't the only thing on Diefenbaker's mind. Like Humpty Dumpty, the provincial Conservative party had fallen off the wall and was trying to put itself back together again. A leadership convention was called and several people were nominated to run for leader. They all declined. Diefenbaker accepted.

It was a thankless task. Only his wife Edna believed he could actually pull the party together and take a crack at winning the next election. What he needed was not just determination but lots and lots of cash. He sent a request to the leaders of the national party, but they were broke after the demoralizing losses in the 1935 election.

When the provincial election was called, Diefenbaker had rounded up about forty candidates. "One by one my candidates drifted away," he explained, "they had lived through the drought, and the vast majority of them did not have enough money to pay their deposits let alone fight an election." So Diefenbaker, in a major gesture of self-sacrifice for the good of his party, dug into his own pockets to pay for the deposits of twenty-two Conservative candidates. There were fifty-two members in the Saskatchewan legislature, so this meant that even if every single Conservative was elected, they couldn't win the election.

The Liberals, the CCF, and Social Credit all nominated candidates. It was a punch-up between four parties, and the Conservatives were the skinny weaklings – not one member was elected. John, who was running in Arm River, lost to a Liberal by 168 votes. It was his fifth personal defeat.

Diefenbaker offered to resign from the party but was unanimously refused. They respected what he'd tried to do. And besides, there was no one else to turn to. Diefenbaker later wrote: "I had run federally in 1925 and 1926, provincially in 1929, for municipal office in 1933, and again provincially in 1938. Five successive defeats! My wife was not well. My law practice was suffering. I was the leader of a party with no representation in the legislative assembly. What I wanted to do was gradually and responsibly relinquish my political obligations, and devote the rest of my life to the practice of law."

And that's exactly what he would have done, if it hadn't been for a federal Conservative nominating convention in the town of Imperial, Saskatchewan in June of 1939.

∞

John and Edna sit inside their car, a short distance from the Imperial town hall. The motor is running, and Edna, his constant chauffeur, is in the driver's seat.

Diefenbaker has just withdrawn his name from the list of candidates in the nomination meeting inside. There have been too many tries. Too much time spent pursuing his dream. His wife is tired and so is he.

Before they can pull out of town, a local farmer walks up and taps on the window. "I worked very hard for you in the provincial election," the man says, "and I don't want to pay for this advice, but I want it."

John nods and opens the door, stretching his lanky frame into the open air. It turns out that some of the man's cattle have been killed on the CPR right of way. A gate had been left open. The man wants compensation. What should he do? John gives him his free advice, then gets back in the car.

Edna goes ahead about three feet and there's another tap on the window. This time it's Ed Topping, one of the leading Conservatives in the constituency. "There's a hold-up in the convention," he says.

"Well," Diefenbaker replies, "the convention has chosen Kelly."

Ed nods. He looks grim. "There's a mix-up. We want you inside."

Leaving Edna in the car, John gets out and walks toward the hall. Ed won't tell him what the mix-up is. The moment the door to the hall closes behind Diefenbaker, W.B Kelly, who was just voted in as representative, announces to the whole crowd, "I was chosen as the candidate and I therefore move that my withdrawal be accepted and that this convention choose as its candidate John Diefenbaker."

John stands dumbfounded. He has been chosen without even running. The support is unanimous.

Cheers and congratulations rain down on him. A few minutes later John sheepishly slips out of the hall. How will he explain this to Edna, who thinks they are going to live a normal life from now on?

He gets in the car and begins driving towards Prince Albert. He goes down grid roads, the car thumping over the potholes. He doesn't say a word, which is extremely odd for John. Finally, the silence becomes too much. "What happened in there?" Edna asks.

Diefenbaker lets out his breath. "They chose me as their candidate," he says, as quietly as possible.

∞

Edna soon got over the shock, but John was the first to have a sense of humour about it all. The next day in court some of his colleagues asked if a good candidate had been nominated.

"Well," he said, deadpanning, "not very good." When the Saskatoon *Phoenix* came that afternoon it had Diefenbaker's picture in it and revealed him to be the new candidate. Everyone had a good laugh.

The laughter was short-lived. That September, Germany invaded Poland. Canada immediately declared war. By January of 1940 the House of Commons was dissolved and a general election called for March 26th.

4

Member of Parliament

In February Diefenbaker got a lucky political break. He was the court-appointed counsel for the defence of Isobel Emele, a woman who was accused of murdering her pro-Nazi husband. Henry Emele was a tyrant who taunted his wife with such pleasantries as, "Hitler will run this country and you'll learn to like it." He had also twice been convicted of assaulting her. Isobel was charged with shooting her husband through a hole in the kitchen door with a .30 calibre Remington rifle. She claimed Henry had gone mad and committed suicide.

During the trial, Diefenbaker fixed his steely gaze on each of the male jurors as he listed the reasons why

At his House of Commons seat pointing his finger,
a move for which Diefenbaker was famous.
"You strike me to the heart every time you speak,"
Prime Minister Mackenzie King said to Diefenbaker.

this was not murder. Then he went to the exhibit table, grabbed the Remington, and pointed the barrel towards his own chest. "The length of the arms is what counts," he said, his voice echoing through the court-room, "And there is no evidence before this court as to the length of that man's arms." But Diefenbaker was far from done. He reminded the jury that Isobel had just cooked dinner for two before her husband's death. "That does not look like premeditated murder to me!"

The trial ended. The jury returned shortly with two words: "Not guilty." Applause boomed through the courtroom.

Diefenbaker rode that applause right into his elec-tion campaign. He was now seen as an anti-Nazi defender of the downtrodden, exactly what the country needed in wartime.

Diefenbaker switched to political overdrive. He packed in fifty-seven meetings in five weeks, and a fif-teen-minute radio broadcast twice a week. He called for a legislated floor price for wheat, which caught the farmers' attention. He told J.S. Woodsworth, the for-mer leader of the CCF party, exactly what he thought of his pacifism. Diefenbaker travelled by horse and cutter, by train, and by car. He braved blizzards, even spent the night stuck in one. His wife Edna was often by his side and she could break the ice of any conversa-tion.

When Diefenbaker hit the stage he was on fire. His competition asked: "Why would farmers want a lawyer to represent them in Parliament?" Diefenbaker's supporters fought back with a poster saying: "The Liberals are right. John Diefenbaker is a successful lawyer and does get large fees. Farmers, put your case in his hands. It won't cost you anything."

Then the Liberal candidate, J. Fred Johnston, made a mistake. On the Saturday before the election, during a radio broadcast from Regina, he declared, "Are you going to have me as your Member, or are you going to have a conscript? Diefenbaker was a conscript."

Diefenbaker, who was sitting in the station waiting for his turn, saw red. The suggestion that he had to be drafted by the government into joining the troops during World War I was outrageous. He had volunteered. A few minutes later he strode into the studio, sat himself down in front of the microphone and launched into his final address. It was wartime, so every speech was read and approved beforehand by a monitor. The monitor sat across from John, reading along to be sure Diefenbaker didn't stray from his subject and somehow encourage enemy forces. When the monitor turned away for a moment, Diefenbaker interjected, "I've been in many elections, but this is the first time a deliberate lie has been told by anyone against me. I joined up in 1916 and took my commission. I was invalided home in February 1917. Conscription didn't come in until after the election in December 1917, the Unionist election that I participated in. Johnston's statement reflects on everyone who enlisted in the twenty months preceding conscription." The attempt to defame Diefenbaker backfired, and a number of votes swung his way.

But would it be enough?

∽

Election night, March 26, 1940. John Diefenbaker and Edna are sitting in their home in Prince Albert with several guests, including John's law partner Jack Cuelenaere. They're shooting the breeze, unwinding after a gruelling campaign, nervously watching the clock tick down as the votes are counted all across the country. John paces, passing the time by mimicking his opponents. Edna teases him, calling John, "the honourable member." Later she whispers, "This time you will win, my dear." At eleven o' clock John finds out that he's leading by 150 votes. A good margin, but Diefenbaker doesn't want to get his hopes up. By midnight he still hasn't heard the final count – Lake Centre is the only constituency in Saskatchewan in which there are no radio reports. The radio station signs off for the night. Finally, Jack, who is President of the Saskatchewan Young Liberals (Diefenbaker does not mind that his partner has a different political stripe than he does), goes to the phone and contacts his party's headquarters in Regina. "How are we doing?" he asks.

"Fine," the man on the other end answers, "except in Lake Centre, and that's a seat we never expected to lose."

"You mean to tell me we've lost it?"

"Yeah, it's gone."

Diefenbaker can barely contain his happiness. He has won by 280 votes.

John Diefenbaker is heading to Parliament.

∽

On May 10th Germany invaded Holland, Belgium, and Luxembourg. France would be next in line, as Panzer divisions moved quickly into place. On the same day Winston Churchill became prime minister of Great Britain.

The next morning, John Diefenbaker sat in a CNR dining car, rattling its way east. He was waiting for his breakfast to arrive. A man joined him and a moment later Edna arrived, slipping into her seat and smiling warmly.

"Where are you going?" she asked the man.

"I am going to Ottawa," he said.

"Oh, are you going to work for the government?"

"Sort of," he answered.

"Well, my husband will be of great assistance to you because he is going to be prime minister."

The man grinned at the charming, attractive redhead. She obviously loved her husband dearly and had grand dreams about him. "Didn't your husband run quite often?" he asked.

"Five times," she said, happily. "Just like Robert the Bruce! The spider, up and down, up and down. But my husband will help you."

"I don't think he will give me much help," he said, his eyes twinkling with humour, "because I am a Liberal MP."

All three of them broke into laughter. Liberal James Sinclair became a fast friend. Edna reminded him four or five times a day that John was going to be prime minister. Sinclair was so charmed by Edna and her support of John that he changed his own plan to postpone his marriage. (His yet-to-be-born daughter, Margaret Sinclair, would later marry a prime minister: Pierre Elliott Trudeau.)

On their trips to and from Ottawa, John and Edna became a political tag team, with Edna often introducing herself to a stranger and John taking over with jokes and stories. It helped them win a number of hearts and a few more votes too.

The Diefenbakers lived at the Château Laurier and John was given a tiny office. Everywhere he went, Edna was at his side, spreading her bubbly enthusiasm through the press gallery. She often spoke of how "my Johnny" was going to become prime minister. Most people just smiled at her and kept their thoughts to themselves.

∞

The clock on the Peace Tower had stopped. It was the 16th of May, 1940, the first day of Parliament. Diefenbaker was haunted by a feeling of foreboding, almost as if there were a supernatural aura in the air. Canadian troops were training for war, and soldiers were dying across the ocean as the Germans pushed their way into France and forced the French and British armies to retreat; it seemed only fitting that the clock had stopped.

Diefenbaker found his seat in the House of Commons, in the third row on the right, surrounded by other Conservatives. Exactly two sword lengths across the floor sat the governing party – the Liberals. Diefenbaker was in awe of the size and the majesty of the House.

Suddenly there was a heavy knock on the door of the Commons.

"Black Rod," a gruff voice boomed. The door was opened. The Gentleman Usher of the Black Rod took his traditional five steps into the Commons chamber and announced that it was the King's command that all the honourable members of the House follow him to the chamber of the honourable Senate. At the front of their procession was the sergeant-at-arms, with the mace, a symbol of the authority of the House of Commons, over his right shoulder. The MPs followed him through the wide corridor, where crowds watched. They went under the arch below the Peace Tower and into the Red Chamber of the Senate. There the members lined up along the rail because only one of their number was allowed into the Upper Chamber: the prime minister. Mackenzie King sat at the right of the King's representative. The Chief Justice of Canada read the throne speech that officially opened Parliament.

It's a tradition that dates back to the days of Charles I. William Diefenbaker had described it to young John, who now saw it all with his own eyes.

Diefenbaker was in awe of the whole experience of being in Parliament. He explained the feeling in his memoirs: "It has been said that for the first six months a new Member wonders how he ever got elected to such a great institution; thereafter, he wonders how any of the other Members ever got elected."

Soon he had to give his maiden speech. "I felt that I was in a great vacuum, surrounded by a material of one-way transparency: I could see the others in the House, but they could not see me; and perhaps they could not hear me." Despite his jitters he was able to get out a short declaration of patriotism and touch on a theme close to his heart. "I spoke of all those who were proud to wear 'Canada' on the shoulders of their uniforms in the First World War, and of the sense of nationhood, the concept of citizenship that developed." He was especially concerned with the separation of different ethnic groups, some considered more Canadian than others. At the time there were 11½ million Canadians, of British, French, German, Italian, Japanese, Chinese, and various other backgrounds.

It wasn't long before Diefenbaker truly found his voice, using his courtroom tactics in Parliament. Standing tall, seeming tireless, he chastised the government for banning the religion of the Jehovah's Witnesses under the Defence of Canada Regulations, partially because the Witnesses refused to serve in the war. "I took the stand that their religious views should be recognized, that the ban against them should be removed, and that they should not be required to serve in the armed forces in any combative capacity."

John rarely read a prepared speech. He preferred to feed off the crowd. Speaking in the Commons chamber he would often place a pile of notes on his desk about his topic and begin his oration. He would pick up the notes, put them down, sometimes refer to them, other times use them as props during a moment of outrage. Occasionally the papers would fly from his hand and somehow, magically, he would find the one with the point he had to make at the exact moment he needed it.

"You know," he once said, "sometimes I think of a clever phrase during a speech and I start to say it and then I stop and think 'that's taking me down a road I don't want to go' so I change direction, or don't finish the sentence. That way, they can't pin me down. They say: 'Diefenbaker said so-and-so,' and they go and look it up and there's a turn somewhere. They can't catch me out."

And he always stood with one hand on his right hip, pushing back his imaginary barrister's gown.

Often his acerbic wit was levelled straight at Liberal Prime Minister Mackenzie King. "King did not like me," Diefenbaker wrote, "I presume it was because I took a particular interest in him. I lived and cast my ballot in Prince Albert. He was my member of Parliament." And it didn't pay to be Diefenbaker's member of Parliament. He watched King with a hawk-like gaze.

King was a stout man with wispy white hair parted on the side. The top of his head was bald and this made him look slightly like a monk. He was serious, but he had his quirks. He apparently consulted mediums and the spirits to aid in his decisions.

Diefenbaker saw this supernatural side of King in June 1940, when news came over the radio that Paris had just fallen. The leaders of the opposition parties were summoned to the prime minister's little office behind the Commons chamber. Diefenbaker was included in the session as an adviser. The men were led into an even smaller room and King came out wearing a nightshirt. Dick Hanson, the portly, verbose leader of the Opposition, asked, "Prime Minister, is it true as reported on the facilities of the radio this morning that the great city of Paris has fallen to the Hun?"

Mackenzie King's face was pale. "I really cannot say," he answered quietly, "I have not read my dispatches this morning. I worked late on my diary." The dispatches were sent for, brought in, and read. King said nothing. He got up, his face blank. He stepped toward the fireplace and stood transfixed, staring at the clock on the mantel.

The room was silent.

The prime minister of Canada said nothing. He seemed to be staring right through the clock at the future itself.

Finally, he turned and said, "Diefenbaker, we can't lose. We shall win the war."

His prediction, of course, came true.

Nearly a year later Diefenbaker's barbs and criticisms were getting under the PM's skin. "What business have you to be here?" Prime Minister Mackenzie King was standing in his office, staring up at John Diefenbaker, anger tingeing his cheeks red. Diefenbaker had come to his office for a briefing, along with several ministers. "You strike me to the heart every time you speak. In your last speech who did you mention? Did you say what I've done for this country? You spoke of Churchill. Churchill! Did he ever bleed for Canada?"

Diefenbaker's anger bubbled to the surface. "What the hell goes on here?" he asked.

No one answered. Mackenzie King actually had tears in his eyes. His face contorted with rage. Then King suddenly grew as calm as Buddha and said quietly, "I regret this, but something awful has happened. The great British battleship, the *Hood*, has been sunk. Where will we go from here?"

∞

The war waged on, and so did the battle in Canada's Parliament. Diefenbaker pushed for conscription for overseas service. Only volunteers and professional soldiers were being sent overseas; anyone who had been conscripted by the government remained in Canada. More men were needed at the front, but the Liberals had promised Quebec that they would not send conscripts abroad. It was a promise that didn't seem fair to Diefenbaker. Then the Japanese bombed Pearl Harbor and invaded Hong Kong, which led to the surrender of the Canadian contingent there. Canada's government had to act.

Instead, they announced a plebiscite for voters to decide about conscription, a move that would take time. The plebiscite went ahead, and the English-speaking parts of Canada were in favour of releasing the government from its promise while the Quebec voters were opposed. King couldn't decide what to do, so finally he declared that conscripts could be sent overseas and then didn't send anyone. "The government cannot forever procrastinate," Diefenbaker declared, "it cannot forever fight this delaying action, if the morale of the people of Canada is to be maintained." King's government ignored Diefenbaker.

∞

On February 26, 1942, the Liberals made a decision – one that directly affected thousands of Canadians for the worse. On that day the government decreed by order-in-council that all people of Japanese ancestry be uprooted from their homes and businesses. They were considered a threat to national security, even though many had been born in Canada. Diefenbaker fought against the proposal. "To take a whole people and to condemn them as wrongdoers because of race was something I could not accept. The course that was taken against Japanese Canadians was wrong. I said it over and over again. It was considered unbelievable that I would take this stand." He fought, mostly alone, and he failed. The Japanese were moved to camps away from the coastal areas.

By the end of the war it was clear the King government had overreacted. There had not been one case of sedition. Nothing to justify this mass hysteria and the uprooting of Japanese Canadian citizens.

∽

Diefenbaker was getting everyone's attention and making enemies along the way. Occasionally members of the Liberals would mischievously mispronounce his last name. It was the rare radio announcer who could pronounce it properly. Even the *Financial Times* chose to call him "Campbell-Bannerman" after his mother's side of the family instead of Diefenbaker.

And the Conservatives were feeling pressured. Arthur Meighen was their leader again, by default because no one else wanted the job. He was unable to win a by-election and lurked outside the House of Commons, trying to direct the party from there.

He soon grew tired of this, and it was decided that the party needed a new leader. "Was not Moses found in the bulrushes?" Meighen asked, "Why should not we go out and shake those bulrushes to find ourselves a leader?"

The Conservatives started "shaking," and one of the candidates who fell out was John George Diefenbaker.

Unfortunately, a larger candidate tumbled out of the bushes: John Bracken. He was a member of the Progressive party and had been the premier of Manitoba since 1922. He had the backing of Meighen and the old guard of the Conservative party. He would obtain the support of the French Canadians. He was a good speaker and an able politician.

He also couldn't make up his mind whether or not he would run. If he did run, he wanted the party's name to be changed to the Progressive Conservatives.

∽

In Winnipeg on December 9, 1942, the Conservatives gathered in an auditorium for their leadership convention. Would Bracken show? Even Meighen didn't know. Nominations began at 8:00 p.m. Still no Bracken. 8:05. Not a hair of him. Finally, at 8:10, he stormed up to the platform and signed his nomination papers. He received thundering applause from his supporters.

At that moment Diefenbaker knew he couldn't win.

It became a night of comedy. Howard Green, one of the other nominees, stopped in mid-speech, released the microphone, and fainted at the feet of the people behind him.

Diefenbaker, who was up next, felt oddly nervous. He spoke stiffly as he read from a prepared statement, and sweat beaded his forehead. His voice was high-pitched, he seemed meek and mild. The audience watched in amazement. Where was the fiery orator who constantly poked holes in the Liberals' mandates?

The ballots were counted the next day. On the first Bracken was in the lead, Diefenbaker third. On the second, Bracken won by a landslide. A motion was made and adopted without any debate. The Conservatives would now be known as the Progressive Conservatives.

Diefenbaker was disappointed, but in a Saskatoon customs office there was a man who felt it even more – William, John's father. He followed the papers every day and looked for quotes from his son.

He didn't give up hope though. He continued to tell his co-workers that John would be prime minister. When people teased him, he just replied, "Well, some day. You'll see."

Unfortunately, William didn't get to see. On February 12, 1945 he died, at the age of seventy.

And to make matters worse, Edna was becoming ill. She had been on medication for depression for some time, but she now suffered a complete break-down and her beautiful red hair fell out in clumps. She was diagnosed with what today would be called mild depression and obsessive neurosis. Her psychiatrist suggested she recover in a sanatorium at Guelph, and Diefenbaker deferred to his medical advice. In those days mental diseases were a source of shame and fear, so John told few people where Edna was. She stayed at the sanatorium for several months and received five applications of electric shock therapy. She was released in March of 1946, apparently cured, though no official report explained exactly what had cured her.

Meanwhile, the Allies were winning the war, but more troops were needed. In 1944 the Liberals faced a conscription crisis. King fired his minister of national defence for demanding 15,000 troops to be called overseas – Quebec would never agree to that. Then, bowing to pressure from disgruntled ministers inside his cabinet, King committed 16,000 troops to overseas duty. It was a complete reversal that kept his government unified. Diefenbaker could only sit back and laugh. In April of 1945 an election was called for June. John returned to the election campaign, promising to fight for the construction of a South Saskatchewan River Dam that would provide hydroelectric power and irrigation to the area. It'll Be a Dam Site Sooner if John is Elected! was the slogan, coined by his brother Elmer.

⌒

The boundaries in Diefenbaker's riding had been redistributed by the Liberals in an apparent attempt to keep John from coming back to the House. The plan backfired, though, and he won by a landslide. The Liberals were returned to power with a slim majority. The real story of the election was the rise of the CCF, which took third place.

Years passed. The war over, the economy of the country began to click along, and though there was now a Cold War, no real danger threatened Canada. In 1948 Mackenzie King, now in his seventies, resigned the Liberal leadership he had held for twenty-nine years and was replaced by Louis St. Laurent, a well-to-do lawyer from Quebec who had thinning white hair and an almost noble look in his eyes. John Bracken, who had failed to deliver enough votes in the last election, was persuaded to resign the leadership of the Progressive Conservatives.

Once again Diefenbaker stepped up to bat for the leadership. He spoke in Saskatoon, Winnipeg, Vancouver, Toronto, Edmonton, Calgary, Halifax, Saint John, and Montreal in an effort to drum up support. When asked if he would defeat George Drew, his main competition, he answered confidently, "Of course I will." Then he added, "I mean that seriously, although I would not have said it two weeks ago."

∞

On September 30th in the Ottawa Coliseum, the Progressive Conservatives met where hockey players battered each other and pucks scarred the rink walls with black. Diefenbaker gave a twenty-minute speech condemning the communist menace in the world and asking his party to inspire Canadians to work even harder to make Canada better.

It wasn't enough. Drew won on the first ballot, with 827 votes, leaving Diefenbaker in second place with 311. Though he'd gained some popularity, the party members chose a man from the East, closer to the financial powers of Canada.

But John had one more humiliation to endure. "On the night of Drew's victory, I went up to his suite in the Château Laurier. They were celebrating. I was an intruder. I went to congratulate him. I walked into that gathering and it was as if an animal not customarily admitted to homes had suddenly entered the place."

Dejected, John returned to Prince Albert the next day. His only consolation was the messages of support and well wishes from across the country, including one from Paul Martin, the Minister of National Health and Welfare, who felt John had deserved the leadership.

∞

Parliament was dissolved in April of the next year and another election was declared for June. The Liberals, even with a new, untested leader, seemed inevitable winners. Diefenbaker, who was now a veteran campaigner, went from town to town, his main competition being the CCF. He cruised to another victory, but the Conservatives lost even more seats with Drew at the helm.

John travelled to Australia to attend a conference of the Commonwealth Parliamentary Association. While there, he heard reports of a terrible accident in British Columbia: two CNR passenger trains had collided head-on near Canoe River. Wooden passenger cars were crushed by the newer metal cars in a tele-scoping effect. Twenty-one people, mostly Canadian soldiers on their way to Korea, were killed. Alfred John (Jack) Atherton, a young telegraph operator, was blamed for the crash because he allegedly relayed an improper order. He was charged with manslaughter. John thought the case interesting, and knew whoever acted as defence lawyer would have a tough time.

On December 22, 1950, when John's plane landed in Vancouver after his return flight from Australia, he was handed a telegram from the family doctor: "Come at once. Edna seriously ill." He flew to Saskatoon to find Edna in the advanced stages of acute lymphatic leukemia. She had been diagnosed months previously but had chosen not to tell John before he left for his conference.

The only place for John Diefenbaker was beside his wife. When Parliament opened in late January, Diefenbaker's seat was empty. Paul Martin arranged to have an experimental drug from New York imported, but it proved ineffective. All they could do was wait.

Meanwhile, Edna had received a secret visit from Alfred Atherton, the father of the young man charged with manslaughter in the train accident. Alfred had grown up in Diefenbaker's riding and had talked his way in to see Edna.

"Alfred Atherton has been to see me," she told John. "Everyone in the CNR is running away from responsibility for what appears to have been a grievous disregard for human lives." She then told John to take the case. He explained that he'd have to pay the fif-teen-hundred-dollar fee to join the British Columbia bar. He had his duty as an MP to consider, and she was so sick, how could he leave her? Edna didn't waver. "Please John, I told him you would take the case. Jack Atherton is innocent, but his life will be destroyed if he does not have you to defend him. Please take it... for my sake."

"All right Edna," he said. "I will see young Atherton and see if I can win the case."

In early February, Edna Diefenbaker, the woman who had accompanied John to so many meetings, who had driven their car while he slept or prepared his speeches, died. She was buried in Woodlawn Cemetery in Saskatoon. The press across the country remarked on the sad loss of Edna, whom they called an unelected member of Parliament. John felt abandoned and deeply anguished.

But he had a court case to win.

5

Leader of the Opposition

"**A**re you ready for your examination?" The Treasurer of the Law Society stared across the table at Diefenbaker. John had paid the fifteen-hundred-dollar fee to join the British Columbia bar. He now had to take an exam. If he failed, he would have to wait to re-apply and would miss the trial.

"I'm ready."

"Are there contracts required by statute to be in writing?"

John considered the question. Was this the beginning of some sort of legal trap? "Yes," he said.

"Name one of them," the Treasurer boomed.

Diefenbaker Canada Centre/JGD3869 1, 2, 3.

These three photographs capture Diefenbaker the orator,
in the middle of a fiery speech.

John took another moment to think. "A land contract."

The treasurer nodded and suddenly smiled. "You have passed your examination and it will interest you to know that you are the first in the history of the bar of this province to have passed with a mark of one hundred per cent!"

John could only leave, shaking his head and laughing. Within a few days he was in court.

∞

May 9, 1951, Prince George. The Crown's case against Jack Atherton was simple: the young telegrapher had forgotten to include two words in his message to the conductor of the troop train: "At Cedarside." This would have told the conductor to wait at a siding while the eastbound passenger train passed. Atherton insisted he had included the two words.

Diefenbaker called no witnesses. In fact, he sat silently through the beginning stages of the trial. Part of this was due to exhaustion: emotionally he was worn out and still suffering deeply from Edna's death. Studying hard for the case hadn't helped things.

At one point during the trial, his assistant, John Pearkes, whispered, "Everyone's thoroughly fed up. They thought you were a good counsel and you haven't said a word."

Diefenbaker remained tight-lipped. He continued in the same pattern, watching the Crown counsel, Eric Pepler, who was an ex-colonel. Pepler was missing a leg, but he still carried himself with the air of a military man. Witnesses came and went. Still no questions from Diefenbaker.

Then the Crown called an official from the CNR, the man who had decided the order of the cars on the train. Diefenbaker finally stood, and the jury waited in anticipation. "I suppose," Diefenbaker announced in a loud, serious voice, "the reason you put these soldiers in wooden cars with steel cars on either end was so that no matter what they might subsequently find in Korea, they'd always be able to say, 'Well, we had worse than that in Canada.'" As one, the members of the jury sucked in their breath. The galley stood in shock. The Crown counsel glared at Diefenbaker. Finally the judge said Diefenbaker's outburst was improper: it was a statement rather than a question.

"My Lord," Diefenbaker answered, somewhat haughtily, "it was made clear by the elevation of my voice at the end of the sentence that there was a great big question mark on it. This man is an intelligent man. Right up at the top of the hierarchy. It's a long question, but it won't be difficult for him. He'll be able to break it down."

An argument broke out between the judge, Diefenbaker, and the Crown counsel. Was it a proper question? The Crown counsel kept getting hotter and hotter under the collar. "I want to make it clear," Peplar said, his military-trained voice cutting through the courtroom like he was giving an order, "in this case we're not concerned about the deaths of a few privates going to Korea."

He meant that the court case wasn't about the death of the privates, but only concerned the four train crew members had died. Diefenbaker leapt in, glee-fully, sensing the soft spot in the Crown's case. "Oh! Colonel! Oh!" he hissed, glancing over at the jury to be sure they were watching. "You're not concerned about the killing of a few privates? Oh, Colonel!"

There happened to be two veterans from the First World War in the jury. One turned to the other and said, loud enough so the whole courtroom could hear, "Did you hear what that **** said?"

It was the turning point. For the rest of the trial Diefenbaker pretended to be deaf as a post. Every time the prosecutor asked a question, Diefenbaker would say, "I didn't quite hear you, Colonel." The jury became colder and colder towards the Crown and its case.

During his closing arguments Diefenbaker told the jury about a previous incident where a seagull had dropped a fish on a snow-covered line and interrupted a message. Even snow could cause a short in the line. He knew there had been a heavy snowfall the night before the crash, which would have left snow on the telegraph wires. A pause, a moment of silence, was not unusual in the transmission of a message, he claimed. He concluded by saying: "No small men shall be made goats by the strong or the powerful in this country."

The jury acquitted after just forty minutes, and Jack Atherton's mother, dressed in black and sitting in the front row of the galley, sobbed in relief.

The case made headlines across the country. The Prince George *Citizen* even printed the words of a prominent B.C. Liberal who said about Diefenbaker: "For a Conservative, that man seems pretty intelligent."

The accolades were moving, but it was more important to John that he had fulfilled his promise to Edna.

∞

By 1952 the population of Saskatchewan was declining; in fact, it had dropped by 64,000 since 1941. This would have had little bearing on John, except it meant that parliamentary seats in the province would have to be redistributed. There would be one less member going to the House of Commons from Saskatchewan. The job of changing the boundaries was handled by Jimmy Gardiner, who had once been Liberal premier of Saskatchewan but was now the minister of agriculture in the Liberal Federal cabinet. He had no love for Diefenbaker.

Gardiner sliced up Lake Centre constituency with the skill of a surgeon, taking out ninety townships who had voted strongly for Diefenbaker. Then he stitched on Moose Jaw and parts of Regina, two Liberal and CCF strongholds. The Liberals definitely didn't want Diefenbaker back. If he ran in Lake Centre he was guaranteed to lose.

For every action there's an opposite and equal reaction, even in politics. Diefenbaker's supporters heard about the changes and got mad. Then they got even.

Fred Hadley, one of Prince Albert's leading Liberals, invited Diefenbaker to forget about politics and go fishing. You never had to ask John twice to go fishing! They went north to Lac La Ronge along with

Elmer Diefenbaker and Tommy Martin, a Social Credit businessman. They were listening to the American Democratic presidential nomination on the radio when Fred Hadley suddenly popped the question to Diefenbaker: "Why don't you run in Prince Albert?"

"Oh," John replied, "the idea is ridiculous." The group pressed him and promised to help, but John wouldn't decide. They spent the next couple of days fishing and then John returned to Ottawa.

In his memoirs, Diefenbaker explained what happened next: "When the Session recessed in December, I went West. I was met at the airport by Fred Hadley and Ed Jackson (a leading CCFer). Without my knowing of it, Hadley, Martin, and Jackson had been instrumental in organizing a series of Diefenbaker Clubs, made up of members or supporters of all political parties except the Communist, in Prince Albert constituency. The executive reflected the membership at large; it was a mixture of well-known Liberals, CCFers, Social Crediters, and Conservatives. Their slogan: The North Needs John."

Voters rallied to the cry, for they knew John's views on northern development, agriculture, and unhyphenated Canadianism. Nationally, the Conservatives were handed an issue on a golden platter: the Currie report. This was a detailed look at irregularities in domestic military spending. There were over a hundred improprieties. The claim of fraud that immediately stuck in the public's mind was that horses were hired and placed on the payroll of the military. Though this was never proven, it left the Liberal government looking like stooges.

The next election was called for August 10, 1952. In Prince Albert, John Diefenbaker won by just over three thousand votes. Three thousand and one to be exact.

Jimmy Gardiner's "Jimmymandering" had failed.

∞

And, unbeknownst to most of John's relatives and friends, he had become engaged. Purely by a chance of fate, in Ottawa, he had met Olive Freeman Palmer, the minister's daughter he had once asked on a date in 1921. Her husband had passed away, leaving her with a daughter. She was now a senior civil servant with the Ontario Ministry of Education in Toronto, a strong, serious woman who immediately lent her support to John's career and his personal life. "When we met again after all the years," John later explained, "we started to talk about the things we talked about so many years before." The talking led to love and a secretive courtship. In December of 1953 John and Olive had a small, quiet marriage in the study of the Reverend Charles G. Stone, in Park Road Baptist Church, Toronto. The wedding was followed by a brief honeymoon in Mexico.

By 1955 the Liberal government had grown grey and tired. Louis St Laurent was drained after seven years in office, and C.D Howe, his most prominent and outspoken minister, had grand plans: he wanted to build a natural gas pipeline from Alberta to eastern Canada. All parties thought it was a good idea, but the Conservatives insisted it be built by a Canadian company (the government was in negotiation with an

American company) and the CCF wanted the pipeline publicly owned.

This was too much argument for Howe. He was in a hurry. He served notice of closure before the bill could be debated. The howls of outrage echoed up and down the halls of the Parliament Buildings. Democracy was all about debate. This was a dictatorship, some cried. For five weeks straight the opposition parties banded together to slow down the work of Parliament. As the roar grew, the prime minister sat reading a book. The bill was passed, but the government looked like bullies now.

❧

Unfortunately, the Conservatives were hurting too. George Drew, their leader, had to withdraw at the urging of his wife and doctor. He was feeling the effect of too much strain and exhaustion and was now ill with meningitis. The party would need a new leader.

It was pretty obvious who it should be. Diefenbaker had won the nationally acclaimed Atherton law case. He was the most visible of all the Conservatives, constantly lashing out at the government. National opinion polls gave him the leadership in a walk. The backing of other party members swung behind him. And more importantly, funds began to flow in to his campaign from Conservative supporters across the country.

Diefenbaker announced his candidacy with these words. "I have not sought for myself and I shall not seek the high honour of leadership. But if Canadians generally believe that I have a contribution to make, if it is their wish that I let my name stand at the leadership convention, I am willing."

He was playing coy. He knew the party wanted him. And he had faith the voters wanted him too.

∞

December 13, 1956. In the Ottawa Coliseum, the scene of John's previous defeat, 1472 delegates are gathered in their seats, badges on their chests. They are letting balloons go and waving banners and placards: Youth for John Diefenbaker, Manitoba for John Diefenbaker, Ontario for John Diefenbaker. It is hoopla at its finest, an American-style political celebration. You'd think someone had just scored a game-winning goal.

Then a voice booms, introducing, "a candidate for the leadership of this great party and the future prime minister of Canada, John Diefenbaker of Prince Albert, Saskatchewan!"

"John... John... John," his followers chant.

The next day, Diefenbaker wins on the first ballot, with more votes than both his opponents put together. The delegates jump to their feet. Wave after wave of Diefenbaker signs are thrust skyward.

Diefenbaker, dressed in a navy suit and wearing a red rose, comes to the front. His competitors, Donald Fleming and Davie Fulton, are at his side in a show of solidarity. They raise John's arms as if he has just won a championship boxing match. Between them is a man who has battled in the court and in the House of

Commons. His eyes are ablaze. He is sixty-one years of age, but he feels forty.

Diefenbaker strides to the podium and, feeding on the crowd's adoration, he promises, "We will be the next government. We have an appointment with Destiny." He ends his speech by saying, "I will make mistakes, but I hope it will be said of me when I give up the highest honour that you can confer on any man, as was said of another in public service: 'He wasn't always right; sometimes he was on the wrong side, but never on the side of wrong.' That is my dedication; that is my humble declaration."

There is only one sour note. Upset that Diefenbaker hadn't chosen someone from Quebec to second his nomination, a good many of the Quebec delegates walk out of the Coliseum when Diefenbaker's election is declared unanimous.

Diefenbaker immediately began touring across the country and making speeches. A wave of hysteria – a Diefenmania – swept the party. Diefenbaker thundered like a prophet about the downfall of the smug Liberal government. He became known affectionately as "Dief" and "Dief the Chief."

And in the House of Commons "the Chief" took charge. He raged over taxation and low pensions for seniors. He told the government they needed to provide more help for the poorer provinces. At one point during debate he rose, pushed aside his chair to make room, and stood with his right hand on his hip. "What does the government do?" he asked, his voice booming. Out would launch the accusing finger, pointing straight at Louis St Laurent like he had caught some petty thief in the middle of a crime. "It continues its policy of being resolute in irresolution."

By the time the election was called, support had snowballed. It's Time For a Diefenbaker Government was the Conservatives' slogan. No longer were they the Conservatives who had been tainted by their years in office during the Dirty Thirties. They were brash. Confident. They had a new man to lead the charge, a man who might even be bigger than the party itself.

And Diefenbaker had refined his message for the Canadian people. Canada needed a new vision, like the vision of the railway that bound the country together so many years before. The Conservatives would bring that new vision to reality, by launching a national policy of development for the northern areas – the New Frontier Policy. "The North, with all its vast resources of hidden wealth – the wonder and the challenge of the North must become our national consciousness." Diefenbaker had seen the North for himself, fished her waters, flown over hectare after hectare of trees and resources. It was all there for the taking.

The Conservatives would also reduce taxes, get fair prices for farmers, and increase old age pensions. A golden age was coming, but it couldn't be ushered in by tired, old Liberals who had held power so long they had forgotten how to dream up anything new.

With each speech the crowds grew larger and louder. Diefenbaker stopped everywhere, with Olive constantly beside him. He was shaking hands, making speeches, making jokes. He won the hearts of the people. He was one of them. From the Prairies, not some bureaucrat. Things would change if we voted for him.

Of course, to win the election was still unthinkable. But his last prediction in the town of Nipawin, Saskatchewan was this: "On Monday I'll be prime minister."

The crowd went crazy.

∽

June 10, 1957, election day. The streets of Prince Albert were slick with a light rain. The weather was cool – the kind of day where you wrapped your coat tightly around yourself. John was up early, and he and Olive walked the three blocks to the nearest poll to mark an X beside his own name. Afterwards, he wandered up and down Central Street shaking hands and greeting old friends. He had an uncanny knack for remembering people's names, even if he hadn't seen them for years.

In the afternoon he had a nap.

Then he and several guests sat in front of the Diefenbakers' radio, tuned to CBC. The results came flooding in. The Conservatives had gained in each province. Even better news was that eight current ministers had lost their seats, including C.D. Howe. "These Cabinet ministers are going down like flies," John said, grinning. He couldn't help but grow more excited and hopeful. In his home-town riding he won by 6500 votes. It looked like the Conservatives would win a minority at least.

Unfortunately there was no link to network television in Prince Albert. If they won, or lost, John would have to make a speech. So he caught a Canadian Pacific flight to Regina and listened to the pilot's radio for results. Dief had two speeches in his hand – one if he won, the other if he lost. Halfway to Regina he drew a line through the loser's draft. Not all the polls had reported in, but he had won a minority government. Twenty-two years of Liberal rule had come to a crashing halt.

He landed in Regina and was ushered to the TV studio. Staring straight into the camera, he fixed all of Canada in his gaze. He spoke solemnly: "I now give you my pledge that we shall stand by the principle which we have enunciated during this election campaign. Our task is not finished. In many respects it has only just begun. I am sure that you will agree with me that conservatism has risen once again to the challenge of a great moment in our nation's history. In answering that challenge we have done our best to express in word and action what we believe to be the will of millions of Canadians from the Atlantic to the Pacific."

The next day Louis St. Laurent phoned to offer congratulations and say he would be resigning. John Diefenbaker was assured of being the thirteenth prime minister of Canada.

John drove to Saskatoon to visit his ailing mother at the University Hospital. He was bubbling with excitement – one part the sixty-year-old man, the other part the nine-year-old boy who had declared his dream so long ago. When he told her the news she said, "This is quite a thing, isn't it?" Then she lectured John: "Do not forget the poor and afflicted. Do the best you can as long as you can."

And she never mentioned the fact that he had become prime minister to him again. It was not in her Scottish nature to brag about his deeds.

But the feeling of disappointment caused by his mother's reaction did not last long. These were heady days. He was the prime minister-elect. People wanted his time. His phone rang constantly. He had mountains of work.

So he did what any man of the North would do in this situation. He went fishing on Lac La Ronge.

At the end of the day, he ambled off the boat and held up his catch for the onlookers.

"Not much of a fish you caught there, eh?" one of his friends asked.

"No," Diefenbaker replied, grinning, his eyes alight with a mischievous glint. "I caught the big one yesterday."

John Diefenbaker greets Queen Elizabeth II
and Prince Philip in 1959.

John & Olive Diefenbaker take a moment to enjoy the garden at
24 Sussex Drive. "It's a fairy place," he tells his mother in a letter.

6

Prime Minister of Canada

"**D**on't they know who I am?" Diefenbaker shouted, his face tinged red with anger. "I'm the new prime minister!"

He was standing in the Saskatoon airport and had just found out his luggage was in the Prince Albert airport. He and Olive caught a TCA flight to Ottawa, and John soon stopped his grumbling. But the minor temper tantrum made the *Globe* the next day and John learned a quick lesson. Every move was being watched.

On the evening of Monday, June 17, 1957, John, wearing a double-breasted suit and a black homburg, stepped out of a taxi in front of Rideau Hall. He strode inside and was formally asked by the Governor General to form a new government.

The next morning a telegram from his brother Elmer was waiting at Diefenbaker's House of Commons office: *Congratulations on the occasion of a dream at the tender age of six at last coming true.* The story of John's young ambition was part of the Diefenbaker family's folklore (though John believed he was eight or nine when he declared his ambition to become prime minister).

Three days later John was back in Rideau Hall with thirteen jubilant Tories at his side for the official swearing in as the new Government of Canada. "I, John George Diefenbaker, do solemnly swear that I will serve Her Majesty truly and faithfully in the Place of Her Council in this, Her Majesty's Dominion of Canada." He bent down and kissed the ceremonial Bible and finished by whispering, "So help me God."

Diefenbaker picked his cabinet, assigning sixteen ministers to be the new face of the government. He gave the men who had opposed him in the leadership election two of the most important posts: Davie Fulton became Minister of Justice and Donald Fleming Finance Minister. He also included a woman in cabinet: Ellen Fairclough became Secretary of State.

The new cabinet immediately approved the construction of a highway in northwest British Columbia, the first step in the Conservatives' promised development of the North. Next the government signed an extension to a previous agreement with the U.S. that gave the United States air force the permission to carry air to air atomic weapons in the skies over Canada if any hostile aircraft showed up.

Then John was on a plane to London for the Commonwealth Conference, a meeting of prime ministers from around the British Commonwealth. The boy from Prince Albert was going to mix with leaders from around the world.

It was a heady time for John. Twice he met with one of his idols: Winston Churchill. Churchill, who was now eighty-two and liked to smoke cigars and consume champagne and brandy, invited Diefenbaker to have a snifter of Napolean brandy.

"Will you have shome?" Churchill asked in his heavy accent.

"I'm a teetotaler," Diefenbaker replied.

Churchill tapped on his hearing aid.

"I'm a teetotaler," Diefenbaker repeated.

Churchill's eyes widened as if John had just admitted a dreadful sin. "Are you a prohibitionist?"

"No, I have never been a prohibitionist."

Churchill paused, thought for a second, then answered, "Ah, I see, you only hurt yourself."

Later, Churchill gave Diefenbaker the biggest compliment of his life. He said Diefenbaker's election was "the most important event since the end of the war."

Next Diefenbaker was off to visit Queen Elizabeth and tour Windsor Castle. Then he attended the Commonwealth meetings for eight days of discussion about Commonwealth trading practices and international issues. Diefenbaker chipped in with an announcement that he intended to call a Commonwealth trade conference in Ottawa. He was on top of the world.

When he returned to Canada he and Olive moved into 24 Sussex Drive, the prime minister's home, which has a beautiful view of the Ottawa River.

"It's a fairy place," he told his mother in a letter.

∞

Things got even busier. On October 14, 1957, the whole country watched on CBC television as young Queen Elizabeth II opened the House of Commons. Diefenbaker sat to her right, looking smart in his suit, his tie tightly knotted. It was like a fancy ball. Uniformed men stood and listened, senators in judicial robes sat in their seats, and women wore evening dresses. Elmer Diefenbaker, watching from the Governor General's box, was overwhelmed. "The Queen was beautiful, radiant, and indeed she had a regal appearance," he wrote in his journal, "It was a great sight to see her and Prince Philip seated in the Senate Chamber."

Then John was off to Washington with the Queen, where he met President Dwight Eisenhower. "Ike," as he was known, was a five star World War II general and supreme commander of the Allied Expeditionary Force during D-Day, the most powerful force ever assembled under one man. Just five years older than Diefenbaker, Ike came from a western farm background. The two hit it off at once and talked equally enthusiastically about fishing and politics.

"Subservience is not an essential in the cooperation of Canada and the United States," Diefenbaker later wrote, "I might add that President Eisenhower and I were from our first meeting on an 'Ike and John' basis and that we were as close as the nearest telephone."

∽

Diefenbaker's hobnobbing and travelling was far from over. Next he was in Paris to meet with the NATO heads of government. Then back to Saskatoon to celebrate Christmas Day in a private railway car at the CNR station. His mother was chauffeured over from the University Hospital in an ambulance to join John, Olive, and Elmer for a catered meal.

It was a special moment for John and a sign that destiny was on his side. After all, nearly fifty years before, he had sold a paper to Prime Minister Wilfrid Laurier on this exact spot.

∽

Soon John was back at 24 Sussex Drive. This is how he would start his day: "On a normal morning, as Prime Minister, I would get up at half past five or a quarter to six. On first rising, I would have half a grapefruit or an orange and coffee. Then I would dictate memoranda, letters, etc…, for an hour or so before I set off on my morning walk. I did not have security guards to follow me wherever I went; I've never had them. I would try for a mile and half each day, at about 140 to 160 paces a minute. When I returned home, my wife would join me at breakfast. I arrived at the office, ready for the day ahead, by eight o' clock."

And he kept himself busy during the working day. The Diefenbaker government (the ruling party no longer referred to itself as a Conservative government but preferred to use their popular leader's name) got out its pen and began signing bills: old age pensions increased. Cash advances were given to farmers who were storing their grain. Home building loans flew out the door. Income taxes for 4.5 million Canadians were reduced. They entered into negotiations with the government of Saskatchewan to begin building the South Saskatchewan Dam – it was a dam sight sooner under John! And the Conservatives showed they had a few socialist leanings: the Diefenbaker government introduced a federal/provincial hospital program, partly inspired by Tommy Douglas, the CCFer who was turning Saskatchewan's prospects around. This was a first small step towards medicare.

The Conservatives had said they would work hard and they were doing it. John fulfilled one of his campaign promises to the First Nations people by appointing Canada's first native Senator, James Gladstone of the Blood reserve in Alberta.

But Diefenbaker's appointment with destiny wasn't quite complete: he was the prime minister of a minority government. In the Gallup polls the popularity of the PC party was rising. None of the opposing parties dared shake the boat with a vote of nonconfidence.

Then the face of the Liberal Opposition changed. Louis St. Laurent, tired of politics, stepped down. His replacement was Lester B. Pearson, a diplomat who had just won the 1957 Nobel Prize for Peace for his part in dreaming up the United Nations Emergency Force, a contingent of peacekeeping troops. Pearson was two years younger than Diefenbaker and had been nicknamed Mike during World War I, because his flying instructor thought Lester didn't sound tough enough. Though a cautious and thoughtful man, Mike was given some bad advice by St Laurent and C.D. Howe: they told him to take on Diefenbaker.

Pearson came into the House of Commons on his first day with both guns blazing. He lambasted the government for trade deficits, for an economic downswing in the country. He said that Canadians were worried about their futures. Then he told the Conservatives to implement Liberal policies, and finally he invited them all to resign.

That would mean the Liberals would be back in control without an election. It was an arrogant speech. Even Pearson's own party members sat in silence and dread. Mike returned to his seat, checking to be sure his bow tie was still straight.

"This is it," Diefenbaker whispered.

He stood, bringing himself to his full height, clutching loose foolscap in one hand and jabbing his finger with the other, his wattles shaking with anger. He went on a two-hour tirade, unleashing his full fury on Pearson. With each word the new party leader slouched further into his desk, his face pale.

Then Diefenbaker brought out his ace – a report prepared by the Liberals before the election that said a recession was imminent. The Liberals had kept this hidden from the Canadian people. They had known a slowdown was coming and were now trying to blame the Conservatives.

"You concealed the facts," Diefenbaker accused, "that is what you did. What plans did you make? Where was that shelf of works that was going to be made available whenever conditions should deteriorate?"

When he was finished, a dejected Pearson, his shoulders slumped, slipped out of the House. Diefenbaker's followers had a reason to cheer.

Not everyone cheered, though. Colin Cameron, an elderly CCF member from Nanaimo, said about Diefenbaker's display: "I wonder if he should have rushed with such relish into the abattoir. When I saw him bring whole batteries of guided missiles of vitriol and invective in order to shoot one forlorn sitting-duck; a sitting-duck, indeed, already crippled with a self-inflicted wound – I wondered if the Prime Minister believes in the humane slaughter of animals."

The "Chief" brushed off the criticisms. Now he had a reason to call a new election. On February 1, 1958, with the approval of the Governor General, Diefenbaker rose and announced that Parliament was dissolved.

He wouldn't be the Liberals' whipping boy any longer.

7

Follow John!

Take everything that had happened in Diefenbaker's previous election campaign and multiply it by ten. This time the audiences were ten times louder. The vehement speeches were ten times longer. Diefenbaker's 1958 campaign actually worked voters into a frenzy. Crowds broke down the doors at the Winnipeg Auditorium and filed into a building already stuffed to the rafters with people. The trains and planes of the Conservative party passed through every region of Canada. Diefenbaker shook thousands upon thousands of hands.

It was winter, traditionally the worst time to campaign, but Diefenbaker warmed the hearts of

The Avro Arrow, a supersonic, delta-winged interceptor
aircraft, designed and constructed by Canadians.
The Diefenbaker government's decision to cancel
the Arrow was highly controversial.

Diefenbaker proudly displaying the Bill of Rights.

Canadians with his fiery speeches. He sounded more and more like a prophet: he spoke glowingly of The New Frontier Policy. The North would be opened. It would bear riches. There would be roads to these new resources. And jobs.

John was fond of saying, "I don't campaign, I just visit with the people." This was the biggest visit in Canadian history, and the people seemed to enjoy their guest.

"One Canada," he told the crowd in Winnipeg, "One Canada, where Canadians will have preserved to them the control of their own economic and political destiny. Sir John A. Macdonald gave his life to this party. He opened the West. He saw Canada from east to west. I see a new Canada – a Canada of the North! This is the vision!"

When he was finished, he strode through the crowd. People kneeled and kissed his coat. Not one person. Not two. But many. With tears in their eyes. Canadian politics had never before been like this.

Again and again it happened: people lined up to touch the hem of Diefenbaker's coat. Thousands waited to shake his hand and at times it became so tender he couldn't even use it. In Montreal his train was mobbed, and the crowd wouldn't even let him get out of the car. In Edmonton a blind woman pressed against him in a hotel lobby, saying: "Oh, Mr. Diefenbaker, it's so wonderful to hear your voice."

Diefenbaker had hit a political gold mine. He had become Goliath, and the Liberals didn't even have a stone to throw at him. His posters summed his whole campaign up in two words: Follow John! His wife was beside him, his party behind him. And the people were drawn to him like he was the Pied Piper. In Toronto he remarked on the effect his "visit" with the country was having: "Everywhere I go I see that uplift in people's eyes that comes from raising their sights to see the Vision of Canada in days ahead. Instead of the hopelessness and fear the Liberals generate we have given faith; instead of desperation we offer inspiration."

He voted in Prince Albert on election day, March 31, 1958, then spent his time mainstreeting, seeing familiar friends and faces, and never missing a name or a chance to share an anecdote. It was cold and drizzly, but the rain sizzled when it hit his skin. Eventually he retired to a room in the Avenue Hotel, where he relaxed in his underwear and read Abraham Lincoln's biography as the returns came in.

The victory was stunning. The people had followed John right into their voting booths. The Conservatives had won 208 seats, the Liberals 48, the CCF 8. It was the largest political victory in Canadian history. And at home John mopped up with 16,583 votes – the biggest vote ever recorded by any candidate in Prince Albert.

John Diefenbaker had his majority government. He had control of the reigns of the country. Now everyone waited breathlessly to see where he would steer them.

∞

He chose his cabinet ministers, but due to bad advice, none of the new Quebec members were brought into a cabinet position. In Quebec the voters have a long political memory, and this slight would not be forgotten come the next election.

Diefenbaker faced another problem: there were now so many Conservatives in Parliament that he couldn't keep them all occupied. Many had to be left out of appointments. He didn't even know everyone's name; in fact, he hadn't even met some of the Conservative MPs before. How would he organize such a force into a well-run government? Their numbers were so large they dominated Parliament and sat on both sides of the House, with the opposition parties huddled to the left of the Speaker.

Unemployment reared its ugly head and the Diefenbaker government responded by expanding public works grants and tacking a six-week extension onto unemployment insurance benefits. And they began one of John's pet projects, legislation of a Bill of Rights for Canadians. Next came transportation and grain-growing subsidies intended to aid the farmers.

The closely cropped moustache on Donald Fleming's face began to twitch. As finance minister, his job was to keep a tight grip on all government spending. He began to make noises about the deficit.

Meanwhile, the Cold War was getting hotter: the U.S., Britain, and the Soviet Union were flexing their military muscle by testing their nuclear weapons. They also worked on long- and medium-range missiles, which, if a war started, would be flying both ways over Canadian air space. And the Soviet Union hinted that it planned to absorb Berlin into the Union. At the time, half the German capitol was controlled by the Allied

Forces and half by the Soviets. It was the most likely place for war to start.

In order to improve relations with the outside world, Diefenbaker departed on a world tour of Commonwealth countries. His first stop was London, and a meeting with Prime Minister Macmillan. Diefenbaker was well received by the press and by the six thousand people who packed London's Albert Hall, where he spoke about a new, greater destiny for the Commonwealth. Next he flew to Europe, where he met with Charles de Gaulle, president of France, and then the Canadian prime minister was off to Germany and Rome.

While in Rome, John and Olive met with Pope John the XXIII. He too had just been elected.

"Are you a Catholic?" the Pope asked. Diefenbaker admitted he was a Baptist.

"That's all right," said Pope John, "We are all going to the same place."

Diefenbaker couldn't help but be a little cheeky: "So how does it feel to be Pope anyhow?" he asked.

Pope John laughed. "Well, here I am near the end of the road and on top of the heap." Diefenbaker knew exactly what the pope meant.

The Chief continued on to Pakistan, India, Ceylon, Malaya, Australia, and New Zealand to meet with leaders in each country.

Twelve thousand feet above the Pacific Ocean, John and Olive celebrated their fifth wedding anniversary. All was quiet when the prime minister returned home.

It wouldn't stay that way for long.

∞

Crawford Gordon, stinking of scotch, held a lit cigar in one hand and beat his other hand on the prime minister's desk. He was a large, confident man, used to getting his way. He loudly demanded a guarantee that the Avro Arrow supersonic interceptor program would go ahead.

"You're going to hurt your hand," Diefenbaker pointed out. He couldn't believe that Gordon, the Chief Executive Officer of A.V. Roe Canada, was telling him, the prime minister, what to do. The government wouldn't pour any more money into the Avro Arrow.

"My stockholders are eighteen million Canadians," Diefenbaker barked.

Crawford wasn't impressed. He continued his tirade, waving his cigar and pounding his fist. Diefenbaker threatened to have him removed by force. Again, Crawford demanded a guarantee about the Arrow.

"It's off," Diefenbaker said, calmly.

Gordon spun on his heel and stomped out of the office, cigar ash caught in the swirling air. Soon his face was white as a sheet. He knew in his heart the Arrow would fly no more.

It was a dramatic confrontation between the prime minister and one of the most powerful industrialists in the country. Crawford Gordon and A.V. Roe had built the CF-105, more commonly known as the Avro Arrow. It was a supersonic, delta-winged interceptor aircraft, designed and constructed by Canadians to stop invading Soviet bombers before they reached populated areas. The Arrow, slick and beautiful, was regarded as the world's most advanced fighter and proof that Canadians had the "stuff," the technological know-how to build something great.

Unfortunately, the Soviet Union had already launched their first intercontinental missile, and they had shot Sputnik, humankind's first satellite, into orbit. The space age was here. Military theorists now predicted the Soviets would be sending intercontinental missiles through the skies, not bombers. The Arrow was already outdated and massively expensive. It was projected to add four hundred million dollars a year to the defence budget. And, worse, the government couldn't find any other countries to buy the interceptor.

"There is no purpose in manufacturing horse collars when horses no longer exist," Diefenbaker said. The cancellation of the Arrow hadn't been an easy decision for John. "I had listened to the views of various experts; I had read everything I could find on the subject; I thought about it constantly; and, finally, I prayed for guidance. The buck stopped with me, and I had to decide."

On the morning of February 20, 1959, Diefenbaker announced the immediate cancellation of the Arrow program in the House of Commons.

By 4:10 p.m. a call came across the Avro plant loudspeakers. It was Crawford Gordon himself. "Notice of termination of employment is being given to all employees of Avro Aircraft and Orenda Engines pending a full assessment of the impact of the prime minister's statement on our operation." The company immediately dismissed 14,548 employees. The mass firing was designed to make headlines in the media in order to embarrass the government.

Neither the Conservatives nor A.V. Roe Canada had any plans for alternative programs that would keep this well-trained force of technical workers in Canada. Many went to the United States. The sudden loss of so many jobs was a hard blow to the local economy. Not a good thing to happen in vote-rich Ontario.

Later the existing Arrows were dragged out of their hangars and blowtorched to scrap under the watchful eye of the Department of National Defence. For many years this dismemberment was blamed on Diefenbaker as retribution for Crawford Gordon being such a thorn in his side. "I was the one who was excoriated and condemned," Diefenbaker later wrote. "Every effort was made to place the responsibility entirely on me. I was even reviled for having had the completed Arrow prototypes reduced to scrap when I had no knowledge whatsoever of this action." Mr. Sévigny, who was associate minister of defence, said in *The Ottawa Citizen*, "Frankly, old Diefenbaker was being blamed for something he didn't do. He never gave an order like that. It's logical that it was Mr. Gordon who did it. He was the one who was actually in charge of the show. He was the man responsible."

∞

Either way, the Arrow was gone. Canadian pride had been stung. A month later Diefenbaker announced that Canada would place two batteries of U.S. Bomarc anti-bomber missiles at bases in North Bay, Ontario and La Macaza, Quebec. The Americans would pay for the missiles. Canada would look after the support costs. It would be some time before the batteries were built, but the nuclear-tipped Bomarcs would be vastly cheaper than the Arrow.

What wasn't cheap was the political cost of cancelling the Arrow. It was an end to any voter's innocent belief that the Conservative government could magically turn everything in Canada around. John Diefenbaker, the man who had promised a new dream to Canadians, had been forced to burst the bubble on a smaller Canadian dream.

∞

Diefenbaker and his government still had plenty of promises to fulfill. John succeeded in introducing the Canadian Bill of Rights for the second and final time on July 1, 1960. The bill said: "I am a Canadian, a free Canadian, free to speak without fear, free to worship God in my own way, free to stand for what I think right, free to oppose what I believe wrong, free to choose who shall govern my country. This heritage of freedom I pledge to uphold for myself and all mankind." It was a lofty bill, a legal document that enshrined equality for all Canadians, no matter their ancestral background or religion. It was passed with unanimous approval on second reading and on August 10th was proclaimed into law.

Legislation had also been adopted to give the vote to treaty Indians and Inuit. The Aboriginal Peoples now had a say in Canada's future. Diefenbaker's fight for the underdog continued.

∽

John Diefenbaker lifted up his head. Before him, seated in the United Nations Assembly, were the gathered leaders and representatives from across the world. In John's hands were several sheets with scribbled notes on the typed text. He took a deep breath. He was about to launch into a speech that would be heard worldwide.

Only the night before a very different man had stood in the same spot. Shorter, bullish, and balding, Nikita Krushchev had risen from peasant beginnings to Soviet premier. He delivered a blistering 140-minute denunciation of western colonialism and American military imperialism. Krushchev defiantly declared that he would no longer continue disarmament negotiations unless the secretary general of the United Nations (UN) was replaced by a triumvirate and the UN headquarters moved from New York to Geneva or Vienna. The triumvirate would, of course, include Krushchev himself.

Diefenbaker was the first of the western leaders to reply to Krushchev's demands. He started slowly, saying he had come prepared to discuss problems openly, but that was apparently not in Krushchev's plans. Then Diefenbaker leapt to the attack. "How many human beings have been liberated by the U.S.S.R.?" he demanded, using every nuance of his trained voice. His words echoed in the assembly. "Do we forget how one of the postwar colonies of the U.S.S.R. sought to liberate itself four years ago and with what results?" This brought to mind the failed Hungarian uprising of 1956. "What of Lithuania, Estonia, Latvia? What of the freedom-loving Ukrainians and many other Eastern European peoples which I shall not name for fear of omitting some of them?" Krushchev was not in his seat, but the chief representative of the U.S.S.R., Valerian Zorin, walked out halfway through Diefenbaker's speech.

Diefenbaker continued on, unaffected. "What good can there come from threats to rain rockets or nuclear bombs on other countries, large or small?" He ended with an appeal to peace. "We are not here in this Assembly to win wars of propaganda. We are here to win victories for peace."

When he was finished, Moscow radio and the Russian paper *Izvestia* denounced the speech. Krushchev himself was not unaffected. Diefenbaker later had a chance meeting with the Soviet premier: "I too experienced Krushchev's odd behaviour. When he passed me in the corridor following my speech, he stepped sideways and nearly knocked me down with his shoulder."

Western leaders applauded Diefenbaker's speech. The British prime minister and President Eisenhower both congratulated John.

It was a shining moment on the world stage. Soon that stage would have one more important player. For, on November 8, 1960, John Fitzgerald Kennedy was elected the thirty-fifth president of the United States.

8

Collision Course

Immediately upon hearing the results of the American election (a close one – Kennedy won by just 118,000 votes over Richard Nixon), John Diefenbaker sent off a congratulatory note to the new president.

Then he sat back and waited. No reply.

One week passed. Nothing. Two weeks. Not a thing. Finally, feeling snubbed, John erupted with "Not a bloody word!" Diefenbaker had always been well received by Eisenhower. They had even gone fishing together, but apparently this brash young newcomer didn't have time to reply to America's neighbour in the north. Ottawa's officials spread the word to Kennedy's officials and finally a reply was sent.

John and Olive Diefenbaker with John and Jacqueline Kennedy.
The conflict between these two men would bring about one
of the lowest periods in Canada/U.S. relations.

It was a small thing. But it was just the beginning.

By December, John was worried about something else. He had in his hands an RCMP report that indicated Pierre Sévigny, the associate minister of defence, had been consorting with Gerda Munsinger, a suspected Soviet informant. Sévigny admitted to the dalliance with the woman but promised he had given no state secrets away.

"This must end between you and this woman forthwith, period," Diefenbaker demanded. The relationship ended right there, the woman returned to Germany, and Diefenbaker let the matter drop.

The decision not to fire Sévigny would come back to haunt Diefenbaker six years later.

On March 8, 1961, in London, another meeting of the Commonwealth leaders was held, but this time to discuss something much more important than trade: whether or not South Africa should be allowed to continue its membership in the Commonwealth. The apartheid policy of Hendrik Verwoerd was upsetting the rest of the world and not sitting well with Diefenbaker himself. Apartheid meant no votes for the black majority. Only a year before, South African police had killed sixty-seven blacks in Sharpeville during a riot over apartheid. Others were being jailed daily for speaking out. How could the author of the Bill of

Rights for Canadians refuse blacks in South Africa the same rights?

The white prime ministers, except Diefenbaker, wanted the motion to keep South Africa in the Commonwealth passed without discussion. They hoped things would work out over the long run. The prime ministers from Africa and Asia wanted South Africa expelled.

"It is time for the Commonwealth to draw up a declaration of the principles for which it stands," Diefenbaker said to the press, his jowls shaking. Diefenbaker and his staff wrote up a draft communiqué. It said: "For all Commonwealth Governments, it should be an objective policy to build in their countries a structure of society which offers equality of opportunity for all, irrespective of race, colour or creed."

This was not well received by the South Africans. Verwoed would only sign the communiqué if he could add a paragraph that defended apartheid. Diefenbaker and several other prime ministers refused. The agreement collapsed and the South African prime minister defiantly withdrew his country's application to remain in the Commonwealth and left.

Diefenbaker flew home, and for the first time in a while he received praise in the press. When he reported in the House, compliments came from all parties. He had stuck to his principles. He had not given in to the pressure to compromise.

It was a moment of triumph.

∞

"I have several announcements," young Kennedy said in a news conference a few months later. "One, I would like to announce that I have invited the prime minister of Canada, the Right Honorable John G. Diefen-b*awk*er, to make a brief visit to Washington."

John nearly exploded when he heard the president had mispronounced his name. Kennedy wasn't to blame, he'd asked the correct pronunciation from his staff and that's what they'd told him. But the gaff infuriated Diefenbaker. Was the young man mocking him? Did he know so little about Canada that he couldn't even pronounce the prime minister's name?

Diefenbaker and his cohorts flew south for the meeting at the White House. They were led into the Oval Office. Kennedy guided Diefenbaker to a sofa by the fireplace, and the president sat in his white padded rocking chair. They discussed Canada's trade with China and Cuba. Diefenbaker also pointed out that his cabinet had not yet made a decision about accepting American nuclear weapons on Canadian military bases. They had already signed a deal for the Bomarc missiles but had yet to work out the details of adding the nuclear component to the missiles. That step would make Canada part of the "nuclear" club. Diefenbaker wasn't sure how voters would respond to that, though he agreed that negotiations should and would continue. It was a productive meeting.

Then during lunch Kennedy pointed at a stuffed sailfish on the wall. He'd caught it on his honeymoon.

"Have you ever caught anything better?" he asked.

This was the wrong thing to ask a fisherman. Diefenbaker bragged that he'd just been in Jamaica and caught a 64 kilogram, 2½-metre marlin. He was puffed up and proud as he could get.

"You didn't catch it," Kennedy teased the older man. Diefenbaker replied that he had.

Diefenbaker returned home from the trip and went straight to the House of Commons, where he announced, "To me, this was a revealing and exhilarating experience. The President of the United States has the kind of personality that leaves upon one the impression of a person dedicated to peace, to raising economic standards in all countries and achievement in his day of disarmament of all nations of the world."

Kennedy, on the other hand, told his brother, "I don't want to see that boring son of a bitch again."

That night Diefenbaker went home bubbling with enthusiasm only to find out that his mother, now eighty-six years old, had died. The woman who had given birth to him and encouraged him to become prime minister, was gone.

He flew back to Saskatoon for her funeral. She was buried in the family plot beside her husband.

∞

Cuba was a sore point between Canada and the U.S. During the presidential election the Americans, hoping to squeeze Fidel Castro from power, had declared a trade embargo against the communist country. The Americans were stunned when Canada, believing such action would make Castro more dependent on Krushchev, decided not to support the embargo.

On April 17, 1961, fifteen hundred CIA-trained Cuban exiles, guns in hand, hit the shore of Cuba. Their intention was to topple Castro with the help of the American military. Unfortunately, Kennedy decided not to provide air support, the uprising of the local population never happened, and the infamous Bay of Pigs invasion failed.

Shortly after this fiasco, Kennedy made his first official trip to Ottawa. The U.S. Secret Service insisted that their personnel would guard the president at all times, insinuating the RCMP were not trusted to look after Kennedy, even in the House of Commons. "They want to put men with guns up all over the place!" Diefenbaker barked to his secretary, Bunny Pound, "They're not going to shove me around!"

Diefenbaker was calmed down and the "extra" security allowed, but it set the tone for the meeting. Kennedy's staff also asked the Canadians to have Cuban cigars on hand, because Kennedy loved them and they weren't available in the U.S. because of the trade embargo.

More importantly, Diefenbaker's marlin had just come back from the taxidermist and was mounted on the wall of the prime minister's office.

Air Force One touched down at the Ottawa airport. Upon John and Jackie Kennedy's arrival, Diefenbaker introduced them in mangled French to a crowd of two thousand VIPs and a small army of red-coated RCMP officers.

"I am somewhat encouraged to say a few words in French from having had a chance to listen to the prime minister," Kennedy joked.

The crowd burst into laughter. Diefenbaker smiled, but inside he was burning up. First Kennedy had teased him about the fish. Then the insult of the armed Secret Service personnel, and now this public embarrassment. Who did this boy, who was born with a silver spoon in his mouth, think he was?

A few seconds later Kennedy once again, apparently on purpose, pronounced the prime minister's last name as "Diefenbawker." Enraged, Diefenbaker had no choice but to stand in silence while the president spoke.

Fifty thousand well-wishers turned out to greet the new president on the drive into the city, more than had come to see the Queen. Later, in a tree planting ceremony on the grounds of Government House, Kennedy shovelled a handful of black soil. He had forgotten to bend his knees and he re-injured an old back injury from World War II. It would bother him for two more years.

He now had a constant reminder of his trip to Canada and of old blustery Diefenbaker.

∞

The two leaders retired to Diefenbaker's office. The government secretaries lined the walls in hope of glimpsing this dashing young president, who flirted openly with them.

The moment Kennedy was in his office, Diefenbaker pointed at the gigantic blue marlin mounted on his wall, its grey dull eyes staring at the two men.

"That is big," Kennedy said. "You know I spent fifty thousand dollars trying to catch a fish like that."

"My catch did not cost me anything," Diefenbaker replied.

It was a tiny triumph. He smugly settled himself in the chair behind his big desk, while Kennedy sat in a rocking chair. "I'm ready to go," Kennedy said, and with that they launched into their discussion of Canada/U.S. relations. First Kennedy mentioned the Bay of Pigs, calling it, "a terrible gaffe." He admitted he'd learned some lessons and that the U.S. wasn't going to have any more military action unless seriously provoked. "We would talk to you before doing anything," he promised.

Next they spoke about Canada joining the Organization of American States (OAS), an association of Latin and North American countries. Diefenbaker said no, now was not the right time; Canada didn't want to become involved in arguments that would put them either on the same side as the U.S. or against them.

Then the two leaders spoke about the most sensitive issue: nuclear warheads for the Canadian military. Diefenbaker made no promises.

"It's really important," Kennedy said.

"Well," Diefenbaker said slowly, "there's a lot of opposition. But I'll see if I can turn public opinion around in the next few weeks."

The Americans thought this was a yes – they didn't realize Diefenbaker was being his usual politically coy self.

The 2½-hour meeting was done and Kennedy's back ached. He stood, threw a rolled-up piece of paper in the garbage, and then departed with his aides.

Diefenbaker shut his office door and sat alone. It had been hard bargaining, and he had felt a lot of pressure from this young president. The prime minister paced around his office, eyeing up the fish. That had shown the young brat something, at least.

Then he noticed a crumpled piece of paper in the wastebasket. Diefenbaker picked it up.

It read:

SECRET

May 16th, 1961

WHAT WE WANT FROM THE OTTAWA TRIP
1. To push the Canadians towards an increased commitment to the Alliance for Progress.
2. To push them towards a decision to join the OAS.
3. To push them towards a larger contribution for the India consortium and for foreign aid generally.
4. We want their active support at Geneva and beyond for a more effective monitoring of the borders of Laos and Viet Nam.

Diefenbaker read the whole thing. The first three sentences started with "To push." Here was proof that the American's plan was to come in and bully him.

According to all friendly government protocol Diefenbaker should have returned the piece of paper.

Instead, he had one of his secretaries put it in his confidential filing cabinet, which he called "the vault."

Later that afternoon, his fears were confirmed. Kennedy was to address a joint session of the Senate and the House of Commons. He arrived with his coterie of Secret Service guards, and Diefenbaker escorted him into the House. Kennedy began with a sentence in French, then switched to poking fun at the Canadian Senate in English. Once he had his audience laughing, he launched into another plea for Canada to join the OAS: "Your country and mine are partners in North American affairs. Can we not now become partners in inter-American affairs?" This was a blatant, public effort to get Canada to join the OAS. Diefenbaker had just told him that morning they had no interest in the organization. Was Canada supposed to jump through a hoop every time the Americans said "Jump?" The remainder of Kennedy's speech was a moving plea to keep relations strong between the two countries. "Those whom nature hath so joined together, let no man put asunder."

But that wasn't the final insult for Diefenbaker. That night, at a small dinner party, Kennedy spent most of the evening talking to Lester Pearson, Diefenbaker's political rival. By 10:15 the next morning Diefenbaker was quite happy to see the new president back in Air Force One and off Canadian soil.

∽

Things weren't so good in Canada. Unemployment had risen to 8 per cent. And Diefenbaker's vast vision of national development hadn't come any closer to fruition. Yes, they had built new roads to resources. They had even tabled a budget that projected a twelve-million-dollar surplus. But when the Conservatives had failed to win a seat in the recent Saskatchewan election, where Tommy Douglas and his enthusiastic band of CCFers plowed over the opposition, Diefenbaker had approved acreage payments to farmers that totalled forty-two million dollars. There went the balanced budget.

Then came three by-election defeats in a row, a sign that the Canadian people were growing disenchanted. The economy needed quick stimulation. The Conservatives rewrote the budget once again, and the new target deficit was 286 million.

Finally James E. Coyne, the governor of the Bank of Canada, began to criticize the government for spending beyond its means. Coyne, who had been appointed by the Liberals, could be removed from his position only by Parliament. The Conservatives finally did so, but it was too late; the damage had been done in the public's mind. The government appeared disorganized and reactionary, with no real economic or long-term plan.

Diefenbaker's government did start something that would benefit all Canadians. They appointed Mr. Justice Emmett Hall to look at the feasibility of a national medicare system, inspired by the success of Saskatchewan's medicare system. The Hall Commission recommended a comprehensive universal medical plan for all Canadians. By 1966 the Medical Care Act had been passed into law and all Canadian citizens were entitled to health insurance.

Unfortunately for Diefenbaker, that was in the future. In 1961 he had his back against the wall. The

Liberals looked stronger and were finding more and more Conservative faults to pick at. The CCF had revamped itself into the New Democratic Party (NDP), with Tommy Douglas at its head. Douglas had been the premier of Saskatchewan since 1944. He was a small man with big ideas and a gift of eloquence.

And the revolution was on – the Quiet Revolution, a political and intellectual wind that was changing minds and hearts in Quebec. People in Quebec began to demand more recognition of the French language and culture of their province and greater political autonomy within Canada. But Diefenbaker decided against a royal commission on French-English relations.

Diefenbaker asked his cabinet's advice for an election date. Nearly every member said wait, things were just too much of a mess now. Diefenbaker agreed. The Gallup Poll had his party running behind the Liberals. John had always said, "I never trusted a poll, only dogs know what to do with poles." But this was one poll he had to listen to.

Dissension was beginning to grow inside the Conservative party itself. "We'd probably lose the next election, or we'd take an awful pounding," was the prediction of Dalton Camp, a balding, medium-sized man who was now the party president. He and a growing number of other Conservatives believed the Chief was a liability.

John ignored his detractors from all sides. In mid-April he announced the dissolution of Parliament. The election would be June 18, 1962.

"It will be a tremendous battle," Diefenbaker promised.

John began yet another of his trademark whistle stop campaigns, this time portraying the election as a fight between free enterprise and socialism. To get him from coast to coast, he relied on his chartered Canadian Pacific DC-6B, complete with a private compartment in the back for naps and night flights. Things looked like they'd hold together.

Then President Kennedy hosted a White House dinner for Nobel Prize winners. Lester Pearson was one of the honoured guests. When word got back to Diefenbaker that Kennedy had had a forty-minute private conversation with the Liberal leader, he was livid. This was making Pearson look good in the middle of an election campaign. It was meddling by the Americans. Diefenbaker tore a strip off the American ambassador and threatened to counter this action by producing a secret memorandum that Kennedy had accidentally left in his office. This memo would show Canadians exactly how pushy the Americans were. Later, when he had calmed down, Diefenbaker regretted his words and said he wouldn't mention it again.

Kennedy had now vowed never to meet Diefenbaker face to face again. He unofficially gave his blessing to Lou Harris to aid the Liberal campaign. Harris was a public opinion analyst who had helped Kennedy during his climb to the White House.

On May 3rd Diefenbaker's election campaign went completely off the rails. The Canadian dollar was sinking faster than the *Titanic*. Battered by recession and budget deficit after budget deficit, it slipped to 95 cents. The Bank of Canada was forced to sell 125 million of its foreign reserves to keep the value of the dollar steady. Donald Fleming eventually had the dollar pegged at 92.5 cents U.S. Diefenbaker reluctantly agreed to this action, but said, sadly, "It will cost us the election."

The Liberals made the Conservatives look like they'd fumbled the ball and furthered the insult by printing fake Canadian dollars with Diefenbaker's picture on the front and a value of 92.5 cents. They were called "Diefenbucks" or "Diefendollars."

It was like everything from Diefenbaker's last campaign had been turned inside out and had become his worst nightmare. Those fiery Diefenbaker orations weren't working anymore. In London, Ontario he rambled with a speech far too long and blustery. A third of the crowd walked out. In Vancouver, British Columbia an audience of seven thousand, peppered with protesters, interrupted him constantly and even tried to charge the stage. Only the police headed them off. The people who had kissed his coat in the previous election now had a bad taste in their mouths. In Chelsford, Ontario, a hysterical, ugly mob confronted John and Olive as they made their way to their car. Someone struck Diefenbaker on the head with a placard. Olive, always protective of her husband, jabbed the placard-waving man in the solar plexus with her elbow. "And did he double up!" Diefenbaker later wrote.

But in the end, the real blow had been dealt to John's party.

∞

On election day, June 18, 1962, John and Olive waited for the news inside their personal railway car in Prince Albert. A chill had settled over the town. A sense of foreboding.

In the Atlantic provinces the Conservatives lost a quarter of their seats. In Quebec they won only fourteen seats compared to fifty in the last election. The people remembered the slights of the Diefenbaker government and they spoke with their votes. In Ontario more seats fell. The West held strong, except for British Columbia.

By the next morning, Diefenbaker was left with a patchwork quilt of ridings: 116 seats compared to 100 for the Liberals, with Social Credit and the NDP grabbing the rest. He had been handed a minority government by the Canadian people, and in the process, five of his ministers had fallen to defeat.

Diefenbaker immediately left Prince Albert for Ottawa. His face was greyer, his hands trembled slightly. He was tired, but he couldn't rest. He had a party to reconstruct. A country to run. And the first crisis was the continued devaluation of the dollar. He met with his cabinet ministers, who agreed to a temporary tariff surcharge, and Canada was forced to borrow over a billion U.S. dollars from the International Money Fund. The crisis appeared to be over.

The man from Prince Albert went to the prime minister's residence at 24 Sussex Drive and slept.

9

"Everybody's against me but the people."

A gopher helped bring down the prime minister. John Diefenbaker was at Harrington Lake, taking a well-needed rest in the official cottage of the prime minister. His mind was on other things when he stepped off the flagstone terrace into a gopher's hole. His ankle twisted under him.

Snap.

The pain rushed up his leg. He fell over, hoping it wasn't as bad as it had sounded.

It was. He'd fractured his right ankle. Doctors told him the best thing to do was rest in bed. "Their advice was medically sound," Diefenbaker later wrote, "but politically disastrous."

John Diefenbaker and Lester "Mike" Pearson.
John had no love for the Nobel Prize-winning Pearson.

A bedroom is no place from which to run the country, and the image of a weak old man with a broken ankle was the last thing the struggling government needed. "There was a real change in him," Bunny Pound, his secretary said, "he wanted to stay away from everybody and he didn't want to have any trouble brought to him. He wanted to just sit there in his bed and rumble."

John recovered, but he was forced to use a cane for some time. His government, too, continued to hobble along. The brightest news was that by mid-September it was obvious their emergency measure to stem the bleeding of the dollar had worked. Interest rates even fell.

∞

At 3:45 p.m., on October 22, 1962, an American aircraft touched down at Uplands Airport. The envoy, Livingston Merchant, was carrying an urgent personal message from President Kennedy. He rushed to the East Block to meet with Diefenbaker in the cabinet room.

The news was alarming. The Soviets were placing offensive ballistic missiles in Cuba. Merchant removed several black and white large photographs from his briefcase: aerial shots of the missile sites. Here was clear evidence that enemy nuclear weapons would soon be stationed just fifty-five kilometres from the U.S. At seven o'clock that night Kennedy would address the nation. Kennedy's letter outlined American plans for a naval blockade of Cuba and proposed an immediate meeting of the UN Security Council, where a resolution would be put forth for the removal of offensive weapons in Cuba under UN supervision. He counted on Canada's support.

"Nobody knows what the outcome will be," Merchant said, his voice somber, "If we have to fire on those Soviet vessels, it'll be really war. Then what will the Russians do?"

Diefenbaker was upset. Why hadn't he been consulted? Canada and the United States were part of the North American Aerospace Defence Command (NORAD), and Diefenbaker felt he should be consulted before any military action involving North America. Diefenbaker ended by pledging his support and saying he wouldn't talk publicly about the situation until the next day. Merchant departed.

John watched the president's speech at home. The western world and the Soviets were moving towards what could be a Third World War, and yet Kennedy spoke with calm resolve. Krushchev, who had once referred to Kennedy as "the Boy" during a meeting, found out that the president had a backbone.

A few minutes after the speech was done Diefenbaker's phone rang: It was Pearson suggesting that Diefenbaker might like to make a comment in the House of Commons, which was meeting that night.

Diefenbaker read a memo that had been prepared by External Affairs before the President's speech. He then made the trip to the House. First Diefenbaker appealed for calm. "The only sure way that the world can secure the facts would be through an independent inspection." He then took one of the suggestions from the memo and went on to propose an on-site inspection of Cuba by eight nations. "It will provide an objective answer to what is going on in Cuba." He was casting doubt on the proof the Americans had shown him. He wasn't backing the president up.

The White House went ballistic. Britain, France, and West Germany gave their support to Kennedy. De Gaulle, the French president, had even said he didn't need to see the photographs – the president's word was good enough.

The next day American officials issued a statement saying Canada was supportive. "That young man has got to learn that he is not running the Canadian government!" Diefenbaker exclaimed in frustration.

The Americans expected Canada to go to Defcon 3 alert (Defcon 5 was normal operations, Defcon 0 was a nuclear attack). In the morning the Canadian military leaders, including the minister of defence, Douglas Harkness, met with Diefenbaker hoping to get the official order.

"No, we'd better hold off," Diefenbaker said.

Harkness could barely restrain his anger. "Why, Prime Minister?"

"Oh no. No. We'd better wait."

And so they waited. Diefenbaker didn't want to be seen as just a vassal of the Americans. Nor did he want to alarm the Canadian public or further heighten the danger of war.

The decision didn't sit well with Harkness, a decorated World War II veteran from Calgary East riding. He leapt into silent action. "I decided to put the troops on alert without making any announcement. I ordered the navy to oil up and put out to sea, and the army and air force to go on alert. I told them we'll go ahead and do this anyway, but do it quietly."

The cargo ships still headed for Cuba. Under the water, Soviet submarines entered the Caribbean. Krushchev called the American reaction piracy. Kennedy urged him to show prudence.

That afternoon Kennedy phoned Diefenbaker. He wanted support for the UN proposal and formal authorization of Defcon 3 for the Canadian NORAD forces.

"No, we can't possibly do that. I will have to clear that with cabinet," Diefenbaker said. Then Diefenbaker asked the question that had been burning in the back of his mind, "When were we consulted?"

"You weren't," Kennedy answered.

By Wednesday morning the Soviet ships were within sight of the blockade. Cannons and torpedoes were aimed. The world was on the brink and one twitch could start a nuclear war.

The Soviet ships suddenly stopped dead in the water, just short of the blockade. Kennedy ordered his forces to give the enemy ships every opportunity to go back home.

"We're eyeball to eyeball and I think the other fellow just blinked," said Dean Rusk, Kennedy's secretary of state. The cargo ships circled near the line, and desperate negotiations between Washington, Moscow, and the United Nations began. News that the American forces were now at Defcon 2 (immediate enemy attack expected), spurred Diefenbaker to say to Harkness,

"Oh, well, all right, go ahead… go ahead." Canada was now officially Defcon 3.

"I never did tell him that I'd already done so," Harkness said later.

By six o'clock Friday evening Krushchev had proposed a deal: he'd withdraw the missiles if the U.S. would end the blockade and promise not to invade Cuba.

The next morning an American U-2 spy plane was shot down over Cuba, killing the pilot. Krushchev sent another letter, which took a harder line and demanded more concessions. A second U-2 plane strayed over Soviet territory near Alaska and was sent back to base by Soviet fighters. Kennedy believed the chances of nuclear war were "somewhere between one out of three and even."

Then he hit on the answer. To Krushchev's first letter, he replied that the U.S. would promise not to invade Cuba and would end the blockade. But if there was no answer by Tuesday, the Americans would take immediate action against Cuba.

Diefenbaker later said he believed it was a good chance, "we would all be obliterated in a few days."

But by Sunday news came to Canada that Krushchev had accepted the deal. The standoff was over.

∞

Diefenbaker still hadn't decided whether or not to allow American nuclear weapons on Canadian soil. He was more concerned about political fallout than nuclear fallout. What would the voters think? Would

Canada become a target for the Soviets, if he agreed? He was trapped in a circle of indecision and pressed on every side. Lester Pearson was insisting Canada should accept its commitments to NORAD.

The missile batteries were in place but the actual Bomarc missiles, ordered years before, stood headless and useless. To American defence officials, this was absurd. How do you deter the Soviets with duds? They didn't understand the dithering of the Canadian government. Even worse the Canadian Starfighter bombers in Europe only carried non-nuclear Falcon missiles. But Canada had committed to NATO that it would arm these planes with tactical nuclear weapons.

Then, on January 30, 1963, the American State Department sent out a short press release that lambasted Canada for not allowing the Bomarc-B missiles or the Voodoo jet interceptor planes to carry warheads. It said "an effective continental defence against this common threat is necessary."

To Diefenbaker it was plain and simple American meddling in Canadian affairs.

"We've got our issue now," Diefenbaker said, clutching the document in his hand, "we can call our general election." His fellow Conservatives convinced him to wait.

In the House, the tide was turning. The opposition parties were tired of what they saw as procrastination and postponement. It wouldn't take much to topple the government.

Diefenbaker's Progressive Conservative members watched in fear. Inside their own ranks a rebellion had formed.

It was mid-morning on a Sunday in the blue dining room at 24 Sussex Drive. The air was poisoned. Diefenbaker sat at the centre of the table, backlit by the window. All the cabinet ministers were seated, except Ellen Fairclough, who couldn't attend. Diefenbaker informed them he was considering calling for the dissolution of Parliament that afternoon, in order to prevent a non-confidence vote by the opposition parties. What did everyone think?

George Hees, minister of trade and commerce, spoke first. Hees said the public needed a strong government, which appeared to be a swipe at Diefenbaker. Hees continued by predicting that if an election was called on "the American issue" the Conservatives would be wiped out. The public believed the planes and the Bomarcs should be armed with warheads – to fulfill Canada's military commitment. Yet another swipe at Diefenbaker.

Hees was interrupted. People mumbled.

"Traitor!" someone yelled.

Diefenbaker stared down at the table, his face solemn. "I did not ask for this job; I don't want it, and if I'm not wanted I'll go."

"You might as well know," Harkness said, his voice cold and calm, "that the people of Canada have lost confidence in you, and the Cabinet has lost confidence in you. It is time you went."

Those words created an uproar, as ministers argued and shouted at each other. The stage whispers behind the Chief's back now had become noisy, open rebellion.

Diefenbaker banged the table with his fist. He rose to his feet and struck it again. Everyone fell silent. "Those who are with me stand up, those against me remain seated."

But his colleagues were confused. Were they supporting him personally or were they supporting the dissolution of Parliament? Diefenbaker repeated his sentence.

Nine ministers stood. Eleven remained seated.

"I'm going to tell them to make you prime minister," Diefenbaker whispered to Fleming.

"You can't do that!" he hissed back.

"I propose that Donald Fleming be named prime minister," Diefenbaker announced. "I will leave you to discuss the proposal. I will be in the library." And with that he left.

"Nest of traitors!" Howard Green cried, as he followed Diefenbaker out. Alvin Hamilton yelled, "You treacherous bastards! No prime minister has ever had to deal with so many sons of bitches." Then he was out the door too. Others followed.

The remaining ministers sat in shocked silence. Soon, they realized, history would frown on them. No one loved a Judas. They came up with a memo that read: "The Cabinet expresses its loyalty to the Prime Minister and its willingness to continue to give him full support." They also added that now was not the time for dissolution.

The message was carried to Diefenbaker, who was in the library with Olive, quietly munching away at a sandwich. Happy, his golden retriever, was at his feet. He accepted the note and spoke openly of what might happen if he resigned. Nothing was decided though.

One person did resign. Harkness, the minister of defence, had had enough: "The point was finally reached when I considered that my honour and integrity required that I take this step."

Now the public knew that all was not well in the realm of the Progressive Conservatives. It got worse on February 5, 1963 when the government was defeated. The Opposition members threw shredded paper, cheered, sang, and jeered.

They could barely hear John George Diefenbaker say he would go to the Governor General the next day and ask for dissolution.

Within a week, two more cabinet ministers had resigned. The February 18th *Newsweek* magazine featured Diefenbaker on the cover, an unflattering picture that made him look like the devil incarnate, with jowls caught in mid-shake. The article read: "Elderly female Tory supporters find Diefenbaker's face rugged, kind, pleasant and even soothing; his enemies insist that it is sufficient ground for barring Tory rallies to children under sixteen." Diefenbaker was upset by the tactics, but quipped, "Satan saw my picture in *Newsweek*, and said he never knew he had such opposition in Canada."

Diefenbaker was all the more ready to take an anti-American position in this election campaign. And to prove he was fighting fit, he had two Toronto physicians testify to his good health.

"The 1963 election campaign was one of the more uplifting experiences of my life," Diefenbaker later wrote, "There was no question that everyone was against me but the people."

He returned to his firebrand style. And it worked! The Liberals' margin fell, and Pearson, who felt worn out and ill, watched his popularity drop. Diefenbaker gained energy with each stop.

Then the U.S. defence department released a tract of secret testimony that said the Bomarc missile sites were costly and inefficient, but "they could cause the Soviets to target missiles against them." Diefenbaker responded with glee: "The Liberal party would have us put nuclear warheads on something that's hardly worth scrapping. What's it for? To attract the fire of the intercontinental missiles. North Bay – knocked out! La Macaza – knocked out! Never, never, never, never has there been a revelation equal to this. The whole bottom fell out of the Liberal program today. The Liberal policy is to make Canada a decoy for intercontinental missiles."

And news of the secret document Kennedy had left in Diefenbaker's office was leaked to the papers, though no details were released as to its contents. Newspapers could only speculate that it had something to do with the Americans putting pressure on Canada to accept nuclear weapons on the Bomarcs. Even juicer was the rumour that there was a message in Kennedy's handwriting that said, "what do we do with the SOB now?"

This only added to the public's confusion and apprehension.

Election day came and went. The Liberals took 129 seats, Progressive Conservatives 95, Social Credit

24, and the NDP 19. On Monday, April 22, 1963 Lester Pearson became the new prime minister of Canada.

John Diefenbaker, who had dreamed of being prime minister since he was a boy, would never again sit in that chair.

∽

John and Olive Diefenbaker moved to damp, drafty Stornoway, a large, stone house that the government kept for the leader of the Opposition. Diefenbaker slept in a bed that once belonged to John A. Macdonald. It was lengthened to fit Diefenbaker's lanky frame. On the wall were photographs of Sir John A., along with various Macdonald mementos scattered throughout the room, including notes handwritten by Canada's first prime minister himself.

Diefenbaker would often go for lengthy walks. And his helpers learned never to interrupt him while he was watching the NHL playoffs. Business could wait until hockey was done.

"It is far less work being Leader of the Opposition than Prime Minister," John wrote to his brother, "and I am getting a great deal of rest and also more reading done than has been possible."

∽

On November 22, 1963 Diefenbaker was eating at the common table in the Parliamentary restaurant. People whispered all around him. Something terrible had happened. Finally, his secretary, Bunny Pound, rushed to the table, her face pale. "Kennedy's been shot," she moaned, "he's dead."

"Ohhh…" Diefenbaker said. He breathed in. "That could have been me." John stood, and leaving his meal unfinished, he returned to his office to write a tribute to Kennedy. At 2:30 he spoke in the House: "A tribune of freedom has gone. Whatever the disagreement, to me he stood as the embodiment of freedom not only in his own country, but throughout the world. Canadians, yes, free men everywhere will bow their heads in sorrow.… Free men everywhere mourn. Mankind can ill afford to lose this man at this hour."

That day the nation of Canada mourned for the loss of an American president.

∞

There were still battles to be waged by Diefenbaker. A new Canadian flag was proposed to replace the Red Ensign. Diefenbaker preferred the Union Jack and the Fleur-de-lis on one flag to symbolize French and English Canada. Pearson wanted a design with three maple leaves. Neither got their way. The government finally adopted a red leaf with red bands on either side.

Then, on December 4, 1964, while John was sick in bed, a letter was delivered to him by special messenger. It was from Pearson himself, and it asked for more information about the Munsinger case. The Liberals had fished through all the RCMP files on every MP since 1956 and had come up with the secret file that described the affair between Gerda Munsinger and Pierre Sévigny.

Why had this man, the letter asked, a man who'd had an affair with a Russian spy, been allowed to keep his job? To the Liberals it appeared to be a cover-up.

To John Diefenbaker, the letter looked like black-mail. A week later Diefenbaker confronted the prime minister face to face. He said he had a scandal on him too: a woman had testified in Washington that Pearson was a communist. Pearson dismissed the charges and said, "We should not talk to each other like this, John."

"I didn't write that letter you sent to me, Mike," Diefenbaker replied, then added nastily, "and neither did you."

Pearson admitted that someone else had drafted the letter for him. "You know I am not a politician," he said, "I am a diplomat."

"A diplomat is someone who lies away from home," Diefenbaker said. He turned to leave, then added, "*You* are no diplomat."

Nothing more was said of Munsinger for the time being.

∞

But Diefenbaker was getting tired of his job, and even Olive encouraged him to retire. Would he stay or go? The press asked him daily, and John, who'd inherited his mother's stubbornness, got his back up. "I was so aroused by the necessity of denying to the press my decision to retire that I decided not to retire."

Then came another election call, for November 8, 1965. Diefenbaker gathered his ragtag army around him and somehow held the Conservative party together by sheer force of will. The campaign brought the Chief more energy. After all, there was nothing like visiting with the people.

∞

In front of an old shack on the prairie, near Borden, Saskatchewan, four men stepped out of a car. One raised a camera and clicked away. John Diefenbaker talked to the reporters about blizzards and meeting Gabriel Dumont. "I have these views," he said, seriously, "and you've got to go back to see where they were formed."

The 1965 election solved nothing. A seventy-year-old man, partly deaf, hands shaking slightly, had fought the Liberals to a standstill – they picked up two more seats to rise to 113, while Diefenbaker and the Conservatives claimed 97. Nothing had changed.

But this wasn't good enough for the dissenters in the Progressive Conservative crowd, now headed by Dalton Camp. Follow John became Blame John. Even though Diefenbaker had won three out of five elections, it was the last one that counted. It was time for him to go, his detractors said. The party became polarized between those who wanted John to stay and those who wished he'd quit.

Diefenbaker responded by turning a deaf ear to the criticism and critics. And if the noise was too loud, he'd even turn off his hearing aid.

John continued his endless attacks on the government, each moment a grand performance. Once, when a young Newfoundland member tried to interrupt him,

John shot back with, "When a hunter is after big game, he does not stop for rabbit tracks."

The member slumped in his seat, red faced.

The big game was always the Liberals, and soon he had something to aim at. The justice minister admitted that a Vancouver postal clerk had been dismissed under suspicion of spying for the Soviet Union. He hadn't been charged, but he'd lost his pension and would be under surveillance for the rest of his life. To Diefenbaker, this was an obvious abuse of the man's rights.

The Opposition called for an inquiry. The Liberals gave them one, but not about the postal worker. Instead they focused on the Munsinger case and put a public inquiry into motion. The inquiry dug up all the dirt about Munsinger and Sévigny. The process lasted for three months. When it was finished the final report censured Diefenbaker for failing to dismiss Sévigny. There were no charges, but the mudslinging did its job. Diefenbaker emerged looking like he'd hidden the truth from Canadians.

The day following the report in the *Star* said: "It should now be clear to most Conservatives that they must support Dalton Camp's effort to push Mr. Diefenbaker out of the leadership to prevent further damage to the party and the country."

The battle lines were drawn.

∞

On November 15, 1966, the ballroom of the Château Laurier hotel began to fill with Conservatives. Some of the old-timers were there, but most of the faces were new, young supporters of Dalton Camp. These were the anti-Diefenbaker forces, here to fill the first ten rows of seats two hours before the start of the annual meeting. They had been instructed to neither stand nor clap, to sit on their hands if necessary and to show no emotion when Diefenbaker got up to speak. Those who were there in support of John's continued leadership couldn't find an empty seat.

One of John's associates alerted him that something was up. Without a word, John straightened his back and he and Olive headed into the elevator. He believed he could pull everyone together with a compelling speech.

When he reached the ballroom, he was met with silence. A few of the delegates in the back stood, but no one at the front moved. As John marched through a sullen crowd, the CBC cameras were whirring, a direct television broadcast into living rooms across the nation.

Diefenbaker took the stage and spoke. He had faced hostile audiences before. He talked of unity in the party. No reaction. He gave them his best oratory, his fire and brimstone, but there was not a friendly face to be seen. For a politician who had spent his life living off the love of the audience, this palpable hatred and anger was too much.

"Shut up and sit down," a man cried from the crowd. Diefenbaker was stunned. He finished his speech and received no standing ovation; only a few supporters could be seen clapping in the shadows.

Diefenbaker turned on Dalton Camp and demanded to know why Camp had betrayed the party leader. The crowd began to boo, hoot, and jeer.

"You've earned your fifty cents," John snapped at one of the hecklers, but this only led to more yelling.

"Is this a Conservative meeting?" Diefenbaker demanded. "No leader can stand if he has to turn around to find who's tripping him from behind."

He stepped away from the podium, eyes darting back and forth. He looked old and beaten. The cameras caught his every move.

"I'll quit tomorrow morning," he said.

But when he struggled out of the ballroom, he was suddenly surrounded by all the delegates who had been turned away from their seats. They met him with a cheer.

The next day the *Journal*'s headline was: DIEFENBAKER BOOED AS HE BATTLES FOR POLITICAL LIFE.

A vote was held the next day. Dalton Camp wanted to continue as president of the party, running on a campaign of a leadership review. Arthur Maloney ran against him, explaining that his own campaign was all about Diefenbaker: "When he enters a room, Arthur Maloney stands up! When the day comes that he decides to lay down the mantle of leadership which we gave him, he will do so in a blaze of glory!"

Dalton camp won by a vote of 564 to 502. A resolution was passed announcing a leadership convention. Soon, John would be out of a job.

On the last day of the meeting, three hundred of Diefenbaker's followers surrounded John in the rotunda of the Château. They cheered and chanted, "Lead on, John." Then they guided him through the corridors of the hotel in a show of defiance.

Diefenbaker was caught up in the sudden swell of support. "Fight on, my men," he said, and was met with a roar. When his supporters grew quiet, Diefenbaker continued to quote from an old Scots ballad:

"I am wounded but I am not slain.
I'll lay me down and bleed a while
And then I'll rise and fight again."

He was asked whether he would resign. John stared at the people around him, his blue eyes determined, but near to tears. "No," he whispered. He shook his head.

"The Tories made an awful mistake when they scuttled Diefenbaker," Paul Martin later said. "Deep as my conflicts and competition with him had been, I was so annoyed the night at the Château Laurier when they howled him and booed him. I thought that was a terrible demonstration."

Despite John's brave declarations, everyone, even his closest friends, thought the Chief would resign.

They thought wrong.

10

"Washed up"

It was a good summer for Canada; her hundredth birthday was celebrated all across the land. The celebrations reached their peak at Expo 67 in Montreal, a grand display of Canadian pride for all the world to see. People sang "Canada," a catchy tune penned by Bobby Gimby. There was a feeling this nation could do anything.

On July 21st, Diefenbaker headed to Saskatchewan to attend the dedication of Diefenbaker Lake on the South Saskatchewan River. The dam that had been started by a Diefenbaker government was finally built. The dam was named Gardiner Dam, after Diefenbaker's old foe Jimmy Gardiner, the Liberal

Diefenbaker in his study with McAndy, his dog, 1971.

John was proud of his Scottish heritage. Here
he is at the Glengarry Highland Games in 1975.

who first proposed the idea (though his government of the day had refused to build it). Diefenbaker had to settle with having his name given to the lake formed by the dam. In Saskatoon a park was named after him. And Diefenbaker's old homestead, which had been used as a grain bin, was moved to Regina and set up as a historic site. He was already a legend within his lifetime.

John was upset by his party's adoption of *Deux Nations*, a resolution that said "Canada is composed of two founding peoples with historic rights who have been joined by people from many lands." In an odd twist, Diefenbaker held a news conference to attack the party he led. "When you talk about special status and Two Nations, that proposition will place all Canadians who are of the other racial origins than English and French in a secondary position." He paused. "All through my life one of the things I've tried to do is to bring about in this nation citizenship not dependent on race or colour, blood counts or origin."

∽

On September 9, 1967, in Toronto, Maple Leaf Gardens is shaking with the cacophony of a leadership convention. The hockey arena is stuffed to the rafters with blue banners, balloons, and portraits of all the Conservative leaders since Confederation. Reporters dodge through crowds of PC party members. And in strategic positions there are television cameras. This will be the first national leadership convention to receive TV coverage across Canada.

"Good evening, sports fans," the MC announces, mimicking the NHL broadcasters. The crowd laughs.

Then, suddenly, from behind the doors at the back of the arena, comes a sound of unholy caterwauling: bagpipes! Someone is playing bagpipes back there! The doors swing open, a small army of pipers marches out, and behind them, like a conquering royal couple, stride John and Olive Diefenbaker. John grins like the devil.

The nation watches it all – live.

Diefenbaker takes the stage, his back straight. This is his element – there are people out there who hate him and others who love him. He steps up to the podium. He has the crowd. No hoots or hollers here, no planned anarchy. He speaks solemnly of a party for all Canadians. He seems to be getting younger with every word, his finger jabbing into the air, accusing those who would stand against the great party, who would accept the notion of *Deux Nations*. To Quebec he says, "I shall never agree to second-class citizenship for six million people."

The crowd is his. With jowls shaking he defiantly calls down the Liberal government, predicts their disastrous fall. And finally he talks of one nation, Canada. He will always defend her and his own beliefs. "I have fought for all my life," he intones, putting his soul into the lines, "I am still here!"

☙

The next morning Diefenbaker put his name in for the leadership campaign. He knew he had no chance of winning, but he had never backed down from a fight before. This was the final round.

When the ballots were counted the next day, Diefenbaker was in fifth place. In his box in Maple Leaf Gardens he sank deeper into his seat, suddenly looking older. He went for a short walk with Olive and returned. He did not withdraw. On the second ballot he remained in fifth place with slightly fewer votes. Another walk, but he still didn't withdraw. On the third vote he had lost even more, down to 114. Olive was wearing dark glasses, a few tears ran along her cheek. "That's that," she said, "I think we'd better go and get something to eat, dear."

They rose and left the box; police cleared their way through a back corridor and into a limousine. John scribbled his official withdrawal on a piece of paper: *I hereby withdraw as a candidate for the leadership of the P.C. Party of Canada. Dated Toronto Sept 9/67.* Then he quickly signed it with his long, messy, trademark signature. He handed it to one of his friends, who ran it back to the Gardens.

"I guess I'm all washed up, Olive," John said quietly.

But before Olive could answer, the driver exclaimed, "You'll never be washed up, Chief."

Everyone in the car laughed and suddenly there came singing. It was the Chief doing a rendition of, "When You Come To The End Of A Perfect Day."

Later, he returned to Maple Leaf Gardens. When the voting was over, Robert Stanfield, once premier of Nova Scotia, was the new leader of the Conservative party.

John descended to the podium. His final speech had a warning: "Always remember those who have on their shoulders the mantle of leadership. They are subjected and expected to be subjected to persistent attack. Don't, as the fires of controversy burn around your leader, add gasoline to that fire." His voice was strong as it had ever been. "My course has come to an end. I have fought your battle, and you have given that loyalty that led us to more victories than the party has ever had since the days of Sir John A. Macdonald. In my retiring, I have nothing to withdraw in my desire to see Canada, my country and your country, one nation."

He returned with Olive to his hotel suite.

☙

Soon John and Olive were out of Stornoway. Diefenbaker went to the House for the daily question period, but he was a loner now. The party had moved on without him, except for his few loyalists. Mike Pearson retired from politics in December, and the new Liberal leader was a bright young man by the name of Pierre Elliott Trudeau. Diefenbaker admired Trudeau's intelligence but looked down his nose at the man's dress – he often appeared in the House of Commons wearing sandals and a sports coat, with a fashionable scarf flapping around his neck. By April, Trudeau had dissolved Parliament and announced a June election.

John did not retire from politics. A Carry On, John rally in Prince Albert with fifteen hundred locals, convinced him otherwise. The West still wanted him, and besides, he was born to be in the House. Oddly enough

Diefenbaker found an ally in Trudeau, who endorsed his "one nation" idea.

Diefenbaker's campaign was slowed to a crawl and mostly limited to his riding. He easily held on to his seat, but the PCs were washed under in the wave of "Trudeaumania" that swept the country. The Conservatives won seventy-two seats, twenty-five fewer than the party held when the Chief was in charge. To Diefenbaker's joy, several of those who opposed him at the annual meeting lost their seats, including Dalton Camp. "I gollies," Diefenbaker said again and again as the returns came in, "Isn't this awful."

"The Conservative party," he told national television, "has suffered a calamitous disaster." His eyes were twinkling with triumph as he said it. *I told you so*, he thought.

Over the years the story of his painful exit from the party became a legend. At one point, when asked about Dalton Camp, he responded, "Psychologists have long since determined that nothing is more disturbing for the human mind than for a person to have his victim still around after an assassination."

Forgive and forget were not at the top of Diefenbaker's list.

In time he grew quiet in his seat and only lashed out every once in awhile, with that old Diefenbaker wit and righteous anger.

The air was clear and bright, a perfect September day in Saskatchewan. A dusty haze drifted through the sky;

harvest was in full swing. A crowd had gathered and waited impatiently by a roadside. There was nothing around them to see, no visible reason for them to be there.

Then a *thud thud thud* in the air. A helicopter appeared high in the sky and descended slowly down, blowing dust through the crowd. Women held the hems of their dresses, boys pressed down on their caps.

The helicopter landed, the dust cleared, a door swung open, and out stepped John Diefenbaker. "Good to see you," he said, waving. "How are you?"

This was John's new "heli stop" campaign. Taking the voters by the air. He won the election of 1972. Then in 1974 he ran again, this time without Olive at his side. She was sick in an Ottawa hospital. Diefenbaker won his seat but the Trudeau Liberals secured a majority. Olive recovered, but later suffered a stroke. In December of 1976 she died of a heart attack. The funeral was on Christmas Eve in Ottawa.

Here was a loss John couldn't overcome. He was alone. Desolate. At times he would sit on a hotel bed, stare at her picture and say, "There is nothing now."

But, apparently there was one more thing.

∞

On April 19, 1978, the convention hall of the Sheraton Marlboro Motor hotel in Prince Albert was half filled with 350 people.

"Mr. Diefenbaker, on behalf of this convention, I offer you the nomination. I ask you to accept it, and I invite you to address the meeting."

John Diefenbaker walked to the podium. For the last time he spoke the words: "Mr. President, you have offered me your nomination." He paused, sensing the crowd's anticipation. "I accept."

He was met with a standing ovation. John Diefenbaker would run for the last time. He was now the grand old man of the Conservatives.

A year later, on Friday, April 13th, he was on the campaign trail and having a rest the night after officially opening the Diefenbaker campaign quarters, when he suffered a light stroke. He fell from his bed, struck his head on a night table, and got a black eye in the process. One of his aides, who had been sleeping next door, rushed to his side and helped him back to bed.

The next morning John was unable to rise. He was confused and feeling dizzy. His supporters told the media he had the flu. By that afternoon the press reported he was in a coma. Campaign managers denied it, but Diefenbaker still wasn't recovering. An oxygen tank was brought in and a bland diet recommended by doctors. Still no recovery. By Wednesday, Harry Houghton, one of Dief's supporters, said, "The old man's hungry." By Monday, Houghton stepped in again announcing, "This god damned squirrel food isn't enough!"

Apparently that got the message across. Tuesday morning Diefenbaker was treated to bacon, eggs, toast, jam, and coffee. Midway through the week he was back on the street.

The theme to the 1979 campaign was Diefenbaker, Now More than Ever! News of an imminent national Tory win helped the campaign catch fire.

Diefenbaker won his seat by 4200 votes over the NDP.

Quiet and thoughtful, and looking a little lonely, he wandered the hall that night with a vanilla milkshake in his hand. Only one thought cheered him. He was going back to the House.

In late July he returned to his seat. On August 16th, after thirty-nine years in Parliament and eighty-three years on earth, Diefenbaker died in his study at home in Ottawa.

Epilogue

The Final Whistle Stop Campaign

But Dief came out of Prince Albert
He was raised in the prairie grain
And he always had a hand
for the working man
Dief will be the Chief again.
– lyrics from "Dief Will Be The Chief
Again" by Bob Bossin

The nineteen-gun salute echoed up and down the Ottawa railway station as the train bearing Diefenbaker's body headed west. He had lain in state in the Hall of Honour of the Parliament Buildings for three days, while ten thousand Canadians filed past the open casket to say their farewells. Now, he was going home, his final whistle stop tour.

Diefenbaker Canada Centre/JGD7096.

John Diefenbaker's final place of rest on the banks of the South Saskatchewan River in 1979. Prime Minister Joe Clark performed the eulogy.

As the train moved west, crowds gathered along the tracks to wave goodbye. Sudbury, Winnipeg, Kenora, Melville, Watrous. This was the heart of the land where he had campaigned, and the people he had spoken for and defended came out to see him off. Workmen holding their hats, railway men remembering how he had fought for one lone signaler. Farmers stopped harvest and went to the tracks to say goodbye to the man who had always tried to get them better prices.

In Prince Albert several thousand people crowded into Station Square. Then the train went to Saskatoon, where his casket, draped in the Red Ensign and the Canadian flag, lay in state at Convocation Hall of the University of Saskatchewan. From there it was carried to graveside on a small hill overlooking the South Saskatchewan River. Olive's coffin, draped in back, was beside his.

A wailing song was sung by First Nations members of the Mosquito Band and followed by a piper playing a lament. Then the mournful notes of the last post cut through the air.

"We are not here to pass judgment on John Diefenbaker," Joe Clark, the new prime minister of Canada, said during his eulogy. "We are here to celebrate the frontier strength and spirit of an indomitable man, born to a minority group, raised in a minority region, leader of a minority party, who went on to change the very nature of his country – and to change it permanently." The crowd – friends, family, and supporters – was silent. A soft wind tousled the hair of the young prime minister. "He was much more than a statesman," Clark said. "Statesmen are strangers and John Diefenbaker was personal to most of the people of Canada. He mainstreeted through life." And finally, Clark said, "In a very real sense, his life was Canada. Over eight decades, he spanned our history, from the ox cart on the Prairies to the satellite in space. He shaped much of that history, all of it shaped him. Now that life – that sweep of history – has ended. And we are here today to see John Diefenbaker to his final place of rest."

That afternoon John and Olive were committed to the earth.

∞

Walk out the doors of the Right Honourable John G. Diefenbaker Centre, turn left, and follow the cement path, and you will come to a granite gravestone lying flat on the ground. It is etched with the names of John and Olive Diefenbaker along with the dates of their births and deaths. A simple statement.

But don't be deceived by that plain marker. Diefenbaker isn't dead. As long as there are questions in Parliament in a country called Canada, he still lives, saying, "I gollies" whenever someone gets a good jab in. His spirit is there in the conversations of the prairie people wanting better representation, in the courtroom when a lawyer stands up for the underdog. People loved him or they hated him, but they always had a reaction. And though he was at times full of fury, he also inspired true loyalty.

Whatever Diefenbaker's faults as a prime minister and a person, no one could fault his dedication. No one could forget his passionate nationalism. He was the fighter who never laid down his gloves, the boy who decided at age nine exactly what his destiny would be. Finally, John George Diefenbaker did the one thing few politicians do: he passed from being a historical figure to the status of legend.

Right Honourable John G. Diefenbaker at his desk, 1958.

Chronology of
John George Diefenbaker
(1895-1979)

Compiled by Lynne Bowen

1837
Gabriel Dumont, Métis leader, is born at the Red River Colony.

1867
The British North America Act establishes the Dominion of Canada.

1870
Richard Bedford Bennett (future Canadian prime minister) is born in Hopewell Hill, New Brunswick.

1873
Sir John A. Macdonald, Canada's first prime minister, is defeated in the first general election since Confederation.

1874
William Lyon Mackenzie King (future Canadian prime minister)

DIEFENBAKER AND HIS TIMES	CANADA AND THE WORLD

<table>
<tr><td></td><td>is born in Berlin (Kitchener), Ontario; Arthur Meighen (future Canadian prime minister) is born in Anderson, Ontario.</td></tr>
<tr><td></td><td>The newly formed North West Mounted Police (NWMP) trek from Dufferin, Manitoba to Fort Macleod in the District of Alberta to establish a police presence in the North-West Territories.</td></tr>
<tr><td>

1875
William Diefenbaker (Diefenbaker's father) is born; Mary Bannerman (Diefenbaker's mother) is born.
</td><td></td></tr>
<tr><td></td><td>

1878
Sir John A. Macdonald's Conservative party regains power.

1881
Rapid construction of the newly incorporated Canadian Pacific Railway (CPR) begins.

1882
Louis St. Laurent (future Canadian prime minister) is born in Compton, Quebec.

Robert Koch discovers the tubercle bacillus and demonstrates its role in causing tuberculosis (TB).

1885
The Northwest Rebellion begins at the Battle of Duck Lake; twelve North West Mounted Policemen (NWMP) and six Métis rebels are
</td></tr>
</table>

DIEFENBAKER AND HIS TIMES	CANADA AND THE WORLD

CANADA AND THE WORLD

killed; Métis commander Dumont is wounded.

Canadian Prime Minister John A. Macdonald orders the Canadian army to the territories; they engage the Métis at Batoche; Dumont flees to the United States (U.S.); rebel leader Louis Riel surrenders, is found guilty of treason, and is hanged on November 16 at Regina.

The "Last Spike" ceremony at Craigellachie, B.C. symbolizes the completion of the CPR.

1886
Honore Mercer is elected premier of Quebec on a wave of French Canadian nationalism strengthened by the execution of Louis Riel.

1891
Canada's Prime Minister, Sir John A. Macdonald, dies in office.

1894
William Thomas Diefenbaker, a schoolteacher, marries Mary Bannerman.

1895
John George Diefenbaker is born to William and Mary Diefenbaker on September 18 at Neustadt, Ontario.

1895
Cree outlaw Almighty Voice escapes from the Duck Lake jail and murders a NWMP sergeant.

1896
Liberal Wilfrid Laurier becomes the first Canadian prime minister of French ancestry; Clifford

DIEFENBAKER AND HIS TIMES	CANADA AND THE WORLD
	Sifton, the new minister of the interior, will encourage mass immigration to the prairies.
1897	**1897**
Elmer Diefenbaker, Diefenbaker's brother, is born.	In the last battle between whites and Aboriginal Peoples in North America, Almighty Voice and five others are killed near Batoche.
	The British Empire celebrates Queen Victoria's Diamond Jubilee.
	Laurier is knighted.
	Lester Bowles Pearson (future Canadian prime minister) is born in Newtonbrook, Ontario.
	1899
	The Boer War begins in South Africa; Canada sends troops to support Britain; the war divides Canadians along French and English lines.
	1900
	The mortality rate for TB in Canada is 180 per 100,000.
	1902
	Bob Edwards launches the Calgary *Eye-Opener* newspaper.
1903	**1903**
William Diefenbaker is diagnosed with TB; a doctor advises him to move to a dry prairie climate; he and his family move to the District of Saskatchewan in the North-West Territories.	The Chinese head tax, originally imposed in 1885, rises to $500, preventing Chinese women from joining their immigrant husbands in Canada.

DIEFENBAKER AND HIS TIMES

Gabriel Dumont visits the Diefenbaker home.

c.1904
Diefenbaker tells his mother, "Someday I am going to be prime minister."

1910
After several moves, the Diefenbaker family settles in Saskatoon so the two boys can get a good education; Diefenbaker finds a job as a newspaper boy; he sells Sir Wilfrid Laurier a newspaper.

1911
Diefenbaker is swept up in the federal election campaign; he decides to be a Conservative.

1912
Diefenbaker graduates from Saskatoon Collegiate and enrolls at the University of Saskatchewan.

CANADA AND THE WORLD

1904
"Royal" is added to the name of the North West Mounted Police (RNWMP).

1905
Alberta and Saskatchewan become provinces of the Dominion of Canada.

Ellen Louks Fairclough (future Canadian politician) is born in Hamilton, Ontario.

1910
Laurier's Liberals introduce a bill to establish a Canadian navy; the proposal satisfies neither the English Canadian imperialists nor the French Canadian nationalists.

1911
In an election fought in part over a reciprocal trade treaty with the U.S., Laurier's Liberals lose to Robert Borden's Conservatives.

In the previous ten years, the population of western Canada has grown from 250,000 to 2,000,000 due largely to immigration.

DIEFENBAKER AND HIS TIMES	CANADA AND THE WORLD
	1914
	Britain declares war on Germany; Canada is automatically at war.
	Robert Lorne Stanfield (future Canadian politician) is born in Truro, Nova Scotia.
	Robert Bickerdike's private member's bill to abolish capital punishment is defeated in the Canadian Parliament.
1915	**1915**
The Sheaf, a student newspaper, predicts that Diefenbaker will be the leader of the Opposition in the House of Commons in forty years.	In the U.S., the Ku Klux Klan, a white supremacist outlaw organization, is revived in Atlanta, Georgia.
1916	**1916**
Diefenbaker volunteers for the Canadian Army; with the rank of lieutenant he sails for England.	In Canada, Manitoba is the first province to give women the right to vote.
1917	**1917**
A "disordered action of the heart" makes Diefenbaker unable to serve; he returns to Canada and attempts unsuccessfully to enlist in the Royal Flying Corps; he enrolls in law school at the University of Saskatchewan.	At the Battle of Vimy Ridge in April, Canadian soldiers fight as a unit for the first time and achieve victory where the British and French have failed.
	Conscription divides Canadians along French/English lines and leads to the formation of the Union government.
	In the October Revolution in Russia, the Bolshevik (later the Communist) party seizes power.

DIEFENBAKER AND HIS TIMES	CANADA AND THE WORLD
	1918 World War One ends; a worldwide influenza epidemic kills almost 22 million people in two years.
1919 Diefenbaker completes his law degree and is called to the Saskatchewan bar; he sets up a law office in Wakaw, Saskatchewan.	**1919** In the Winnipeg General Strike, federal troops occupy the city after RNWMP charge a crowd on "Bloody Sunday."
1920 Diefenbaker is able to afford to move into a larger office and buy a Maxwell touring car.	**1920** In Canada, farmers from the Prairies and Ontario unite with dissident Liberals led by Thomas Crerar to form the Progressive party; Arthur Meighen succeeds Borden as prime minister. RNWMP merges with the Dominion Police to form the Royal Canadian Mounted Police (RCMP).
1921 Diefenbaker asks Olive Freeman for a date. Diefenbaker drives his car to Vancouver, B.C. Diefenbaker is elected to city council; the Liberal party invites him to join them, but he declines.	**1921** In Canada, Agnes Macphail is the first woman elected to Parliament; Liberal William Lyon Mackenzie King defeats Meighen and becomes prime minister; the election of the Progressives ends the tradition of the two-party system. The Ku Klux Klan is reported to be active in Montreal.
	1922 In Italy, Mussolini marches on Rome and later forms a fascist government.

DIEFENBAKER AND HIS TIMES	CANADA AND THE WORLD
	The Union of Soviet Socialist Republics (U.S.S.R.) is formed from the Russian empire.
1923	**1923**
Diefenbaker drives his car to Los Angeles, California.	Canada signs its first treaty independent of Britain.
1924	
Diefenbaker's fiancée, Beth Newell, dies of TB; he moves to Prince Albert, Saskatchewan.	
1925	**1925**
In his first official act as a Conservative, Diefenbaker addresses a small meeting; he is unopposed in his bid to be the party's candidate in the October federal election; although he is a lively campaigner and opposes the unpopular views of his party's leader, he loses.	In the Canadian general election in October, Meighen's Conservatives win the most seats but the Progressives support King's Liberals and thereby keep them in power.
	The Ku Klux Klan has established locals all across Canada.
1926	**1926**
In the second election in two years, Diefenbaker runs against Prime Minister King; Diefenbaker is opposed to some of his own party's views and is gaining ground during the campaign until racist remarks in eastern Canada turn the tide in King's favour.	A scandal forces Prime Minister King to seek dissolution of Parliament, but Governor General Viscount Byng refuses; King resigns and Meighen takes power again for three months until he is defeated in another general election; King becomes prime minister again.
	James Garfield (Jimmy) Gardiner is elected premier of Saskatchewan.
	1927
	American organizers of the Ku Klux Klan steal $100,000 of

DIEFENBAKER AND HIS TIMES

1928

At a Liberal meeting during a provincial by-election meeting, Premier Gardiner reluctantly yields the platform to Diefenbaker for ten minutes; the Liberals barely win the by-election; the Conservative party is impressed with Diefenbaker.

1929

Diefenbaker marries Edna May Brower in Toronto; they return to Prince Albert, where his law practice is thriving; he is named King's Counsel.

Diefenbaker switches to provincial politics and runs against the attorney general; the Liberals accuse him of having links to the Ku Klux Klan; although his party wins, Diefenbaker loses by several hundred votes.

1930

Diefenbaker defends John Pasowesty, who is found guilty of murder; the death sentence is commuted to life imprisonment.

Although he is suffering from a gastric ulcer, Diefenbaker defends Alex Wysochan, who is found guilty and is hanged on June 20.

While Diefenbaker is in Toronto on a holiday, the federal Conservatives

CANADA AND THE WORLD

Canadian Klan funds; the Saskatchewan Klan regroups.

1928

West Coast artist Emily Carr exhibits her work in central Canada, establishing herself as a major artist.

1929

In the June Saskatchewan election, the Ku Klux Klan is instrumental in the defeat of the Liberals but soon declines in strength, as does the Klan in the rest of Canada; the Imperial Privy Council declares Canadian women to be legally "persons."

With the collapse of the U.S. Stock Exchange in October, the ten-year-long Great Depression begins.

1930

In Canada, the Conservatives under R.B. Bennett defeat King's Liberals in the August federal election.

DIEFENBAKER AND HIS TIMES

offer him the nomination in the riding of Long Lake, but he is too ill to accept.

1930-1936
In four more murder cases, Diefenbaker hones his courtroom style using his penetrating eyes, his voice, and a thrust of his finger; the hanging of two of his clients strengthens his opposition to the death penalty

1933
Diefenbaker is elected vice-president of the provincial Conservative party; he runs for mayor of Prince Albert but loses.

1935
By now president of the Conservative party in Saskatchewan, Diefenbaker declines the nomination in Prince Albert and supports a farmer as candidate.

CANADA AND THE WORLD

1931
The Statute of Westminster grants Canada full legal freedom from Britain except for amending the Constitution.

1932
Franklin Roosevelt is elected president of the U.S. for the first of four terms.

The Co-operative Commonwealth Federation (CCF) is founded in Calgary.

1933
Adolf Hitler is appointed German Chancellor; he suppresses labour unions and harasses Jews.

1935
In Canada, the RCMP halts the On-to-Ottawa Trek in Regina; in the federal election, King leads a Liberal landslide back into power; the CCF's Tommy Douglas wins his first election; former Saskat-

chewan premier, Jimmy Gardiner, becomes federal minister of agriculture.

1936
Diefenbaker travels to France for a holiday; he visits the Canadian war memorial at Vimy Ridge; he attends the Olympic Games in Berlin.

Diefenbaker becomes leader of the Saskatchewan Conservative party.

1938
In the Saskatchewan election, Diefenbaker runs in Arm River; he pays the deposits of twenty-two candidates, but not one Conservative is elected; the party rejects his offer to resign as leader.

1939
At the Conservative nominating convention for the federal election in Imperial, Saskatchewan, the man chosen to be the candidate steps down in favour of Diefenbaker.

1940
Diefenbaker defends Isobel Emele on the charge of murdering her Nazi-sympathizer husband; she is found not guilty.

In the federal election Diefenbaker wins Lake Centre and wins his seat by 280 votes; he and Edna

1936
The Spanish Civil War begins; Hitler and Mussolini proclaim the Rome-Berlin Axis; Germany hosts the Olympic Games.

1938
Hitler marches into Austria; Britain appeases Germany at Munich.

1939
World War II begins in September; Canada declares war on Germany.

Charles Joseph Clark (future Canadian prime minister) is born in High River, Alberta.

1940
Germany invades Holland, Belgium, Luxembourg, and France.

Winston Churchill becomes Prime Minister of Great Britain.

Prime Minister King calls a snap election for March 26 and wins a

John Diefenbaker

DIEFENBAKER AND HIS TIMES	CANADA AND THE WORLD

move to Ottawa where she is constantly by his side; he takes his seat in the House of Commons on May 16; his speeches are seldom prepared in advance but they reflect his concerns about the equality of all Canadians.

1941
Diefenbaker makes a special point in his speeches of taunting Prime Minister King, who is also his member of Parliament.

1942
Diefenbaker fights against the proposal to remove Japanese residents of British Columbia (B.C.) from their homes.

Diefenbaker runs for the leadership of the Conservatives, but John Bracken, a member of the Progressive party and former premier of Manitoba, wins; the two parties join to become the Progressive Conservative (PC) party.

huge majority; the Unemployment Insurance Act passes.

1941
Japan bombs Pearl Harbor on December 7; U.S., Britain and Canada declare war on Japan

1942
U.S. and Canada forcibly move Japanese citizens inland away from the west coast of North America.

Canada joins the United Nations Relief and Rehabilitation Administration, which aids people displaced by the war.

1944
The D-Day invasion by the Allies under the command of General Eisenhower begins the liberation of Europe on June 6.

In Canada, Prime Minister King introduces family allowances; a conscription crisis again divides Canadians along French/English lines, but is less divisive than the one during World War I.

DIEFENBAKER AND HIS TIMES

1945

William Diefenbaker, having never given up hope that his son would be prime minister, dies.

Edna Diefenbaker is diagnosed with a psychiatric illness and is quietly hospitalized in a Guelph sanatorium.

In the June federal election, Diefenbaker promises to fight for the construction of a South Saskatchewan River Dam and wins by a landslide.

1946

Edna is released from hospital apparently cured.

1948

At the September leadership convention of the PC party, Diefenbaker places second after George Drew; Paul Martin, Liberal minister of national health and welfare, sends best wishes.

1949

In the June federal election, Diefenbaker wins his seat.

CANADA AND THE WORLD

1945

The United Nations (UN) Charter is signed on June 26; Canada is one of the fifty signatories.

Germany surrenders on May 8; the U.S. drops atomic bombs on Japan on August 6 and 9; Japan surrenders on September 2.

Prime Minister King wins a slim majority in the Canadian election; the CCF wins twenty-eight seats.

1946

Winston Churchill uses the term "Iron Curtain" to describe the alienation between the Eastern Bloc and the West that is developing into the Cold War.

1948

In Canada, Louis St. Laurent replaces King as leader of the Liberal party and prime minister; Lester Pearson becomes minister of foreign affairs; John Bracken resigns as leader of the PC party.

1949

In Canada, the St. Laurent Liberals win the federal election; Canada joins the North Atlantic Treaty Organization (NATO).

The South African government establishes apartheid, which prevents the black majority from voting.

DIEFENBAKER AND HIS TIMES	**CANADA AND THE WORLD**

1950

Diefenbaker attends a conference of the Commonwealth Parliamentary Association in Australia; when he returns he receives news that Edna has acute lymphatic leukemia; Paul Martin arranges for an experimental drug to be imported but it proves ineffective.

1950

North Korea invades South Korea; the UN mounts a police action, which Canada supports.

Former Canadian prime minister King dies.

1951

Though near death, Edna pleads with Diefenbaker to defend Alfred John (Jack) Atherton, a telegrapher charged with causing the collision of two passenger trains loaded with troops bound for Korea; he passes the B.C. bar exam and, though tired and stricken with grief, goes to Prince George to successfully defend Atherton.

1951

In Canada, the Massey Commission recommends greater government support of the arts through creation of an arts funding body.

1952

With Jimmy Gardiner in charge of redistribution of parliamentary seats in Saskatchewan, Diefenbaker sees the parts of his riding that support him most strongly removed; a coalition of Liberals, CCFers, Social Crediters, and Conservatives in Prince Albert organize Diefenbaker Clubs and rally around the slogan, The North Needs John; in the August federal election, he wins the seat by 3001 votes.

1952

Dwight D. Eisenhower becomes U.S. president.

King George VI dies and is succeeded by his daughter, who becomes Elizabeth II.

Lester Pearson is president of the UN General Assembly.

1953

Diefenbaker marries his long-ago date Olive Freeman Palmer in Toronto.

1953

Armistice is signed in Korea.

A rocket-powered U.S. plane is flown at more than 1600 mph.

DIEFENBAKER AND HIS TIMES	CANADA AND THE WORLD

CANADA AND THE WORLD

1954

The U.S. tests a hydrogen bomb at Bikini atoll; the U.S. and Canada agree to build the Distant Early Warning (D.E.W.) line across northern Canada.

1956

George Drew resigns as PC party leader; Diefenbaker coyly allows himself to be a candidate for the leadership; on December 14, at the Ottawa Coliseum, he wins on the first ballot; the Quebec delegation is not asked to second his nomination.

1956

Lester Pearson proposes a UN peacekeeping force as a means of easing Britain and France out of Egypt and solving the Suez Crisis; Canada begins to think of itself as a peacekeeping nation.

1957

Diefenbaker tours the country; he becomes known as "Dief" and "Dief the Chief"; support grows.

On June 10, while flying to Regina, Diefenbaker hears over the pilot's radio that the PC party will form a minority government; at the swearing-in on June 22, Ellen Fairclough becomes the first woman appointed to a federal cabinet.

Diefenbaker and Olive move into the prime minister's residence at 24 Sussex Drive.

Diefenbaker attends the Commonwealth Prime Ministers' Conference in London and meets with Winston Churchill and Queen Elizabeth; he visits the U.S., speaks to the UN General

1957

Lester Pearson wins the Nobel Peace Prize.

The U.S.S.R. launches Sputnik I and II, the first earth satellites.

Canada and the U.S. announce the North American Air Defence Agreement (NORAD), which will integrate their air defence forces.

The Canada Council is established to encourage the study, production, and enjoyment of the arts and social sciences.

Canada provides free passage to refugees from the failed Hungarian uprising against Soviet control.

Assembly, and establishes a good relationship with President Eisenhower.

1958

Diefenbaker delivers a two-hour tirade against Pearson and the Opposition Liberals; he calls an election on February 1; his campaign works voters into a frenzy; he promises that his New Frontier Policy will open the North; he wins the election with the largest majority in Canadian history.

Diefenbaker fails to include any of the new members from Quebec in his cabinet; he appoints James Gladstone as the first Aboriginal person to be a senator.

Diefenbaker and Olive leave on a world tour which includes visits to London, France, Germany, Rome, Pakistan, India, Ceylon, Malaya, Australia, and New Zealand.

1959

Diefenbaker makes the difficult decision to cancel the Avro Arrow project; 14,548 people lose their jobs; many go to the U.S.; the U.S. installs Bomarc anti-bomber missiles in Ontario and Quebec.

Diefenbaker appoints Georges Vanier to be the first French Canadian Governor General.

1958

On January 16, Lester Pearson is chosen leader of the Liberals over Paul Martin

Khruschev becomes Chairman of the Council of Ministers in the Union of Soviet Socialist Republics (U.S.S.R.); Sputnik III is launched.

The U.S. launches an earth satellite, Explorer I; National Aeronautics and Space Administration (NASA) is established; in the southern U.S., desegregation of schools is opposed by the Governor of Arkansas.

In Cuba, Communist rebel Fidel Castro begins "total war" against President Batista.

Pope John XXIII is elected.

1959

Castro becomes premier of Cuba.

Pope John XXIII calls the first Ecumenical Council since 1870.

DIEFENBAKER AND HIS TIMES

1960
The Canadian Bill of Rights is passed, enshrining equality for all Canadians; an amendment to the Elections Act guarantees the vote to Aboriginal People.

On September 26, Diefenbaker addresses the UN on disarmament; he challenges the behaviour of the U.S.S.R.; he is denounced by Moscow radio and the newspaper *Isvestia*.

RCMP report to Diefenbaker regarding the affair of associate minister of defence Pierre Sévigny and Gerda Munsinger, a German immigrant, prostitute, and possible security risk; Sévigny assures him that he gave no secrets away; Diefenbaker does not request Sévigny's resignation.

1961
In March, Diefenbaker plays a leadership role at a Commonwealth Prime Ministers Conference in London, which draws up a statement of racial equality aimed particularly at South African apartheid.

The Canadian government decides not to support an American trade embargo against Cuba.

Diefenbaker's mother, Mary, dies.

President Kennedy visits Ottawa in May; the already strained

CANADA AND THE WORLD

1960
Brezhnev becomes President of the U.S.S.R.; the Cold War intensifies as the U.S. admits to aerial reconnaissance flights over the U.S.S.R.

John F. Kennedy is sworn in as President of the U.S.

In Quebec, Jean Lesage and his Liberals defeat the Union Nationale, and the Quiet Revolution begins.

1961
On April 17, Cuban exiles attempt an unsuccessful invasion of Cuba at the Bay of Pigs; President Kennedy takes full responsibility.

The construction of the Berlin Wall divides the Soviet Bloc from Western Europe and intensifies the Cold War.

U.S.S.R. pilot Yuri Gagarin orbits the earth in a satellite; U.S. pilot Alan Shephard makes the first U.S. space flight.

John Diefenbaker

relationship with Diefenbaker worsens further when Kennedy injures his back while planting a symbolic tree.

James Coyne, governor of the Bank of Canada, resigns after criticizing Diefenbaker's government for spending beyond its means.

In Canada, the CCF changes its name to the New Democratic Party (NDP) and elects Tommy Douglas as its leader.

1962

Diefenbaker calls an election; he protests to the U.S. ambassador over Kennedy's apparent support of the Liberals; the Canadian dollar is sinking; Diefenbaker is haunted by budget deficits and recession; the Liberals circulate phony "Diefenbucks"; protesters interrupt his speeches; on election day, June 18, he wins only a minority.

During the Cuban missile crisis, Diefenbaker stalls when asked for support by the Americans; Defence Minister Douglas Harkness orders the Canadian military to Defcon 3 (a degree of military preparedness) despite Diefenbaker's order to wait.

1962

At a dinner for Nobel Prize winners hosted by U.S. President Kennedy, Lester Pearson and the president talk for forty minutes in private.

In October, a standoff between Kennedy and Khrushchev over missiles in Cuba brings the world to the brink of nuclear war; the U.S. has two hundred atomic reactors, the U.S.S.R. has thirty-nine.

In Canada, the last execution of a murderer takes place.

1963

Diefenbaker is unable to decide whether to allow the Bomarc missiles to be armed with nuclear warheads; in January, the U.S. state department criticizes the Canadian government; rebellion grows within PC party ranks; George Hees, minister of trade and commerce, tells Diefenbaker that the

1963

A nuclear testing ban is signed by the U.S., U.S.S.R., and Great Britain.

In Washington, D.C. 200,000 black and white "freedom marchers" demonstrate.

Pope John XXIII dies.

cabinet and the people of Canada have lost confidence in him; Diefenbaker demands and receives an expression of loyalty; only defence minister Harkness resigns.

The government is defeated on two non-confidence motions; Diefenbaker calls an election; two more cabinet ministers (Hees and Sévigny) resign; he attempts to use anti-Bomarc missile information to swing the electorate his way but it fails; the PC party loses the election; Diefenbaker becomes leader of the Opposition and he and Olive move into Stornoway.

1964
Justice Emmett Hall, a classmate of Diefenbaker's, presents his report on a national health scheme for Canada.

A new flag for Canada is introduced into the House of Commons in June; Diefenbaker demands that the flag honour the "founding races" with the Union Jack in the place of honour; in December, by evoking closure, the Liberal government adopts a flag with a red maple leaf and no British references.

1965
In the federal election campaign in November, Diefenbaker is energized but he is seventy years old, partly deaf, and his hands shake;

Lester Pearson becomes the new prime minister of Canada.

U.S. President Kennedy is assassinated in Dallas on November 23, 1963; he is succeeded by Lyndon Baines Johnson.

1964
Dalton Camp becomes national president of the Progressive Conservative Party of Canada.

The UN intervenes to separate Greeks and Turks on the island of Cyprus; Canadian Secretary of State for External Affairs Paul Martin is instrumental in creating the Cyprus UN force.

American civil rights leader Martin Luther King wins the Nobel Peace Prize.

1965
In the U.S., racial violence occurs in Selma, Alabama and the Watts district of Los Angeles; American students demonstrate against the escalating war in Vietnam

John Diefenbaker

the results of the election change the party standings very little.

PC dissenters headed by Dalton Camp demand Diefenbaker's resignation as party leader.

1966
The name of Gerda Munsinger is raised in the House of Commons; a royal commission criticizes Diefenbaker for not demanding Sévigny's resignation in 1960.

Television broadcasts a meeting in the ballroom of the Château Laurier engineered by anti-Diefenbaker forces within the PC party to discredit him; few applaud his fiery speech; he turns on Dalton Camp; the audience boos; the next day, after a close vote, Camp announces a leadership convention, but Diefenbaker does not resign.

1967
In July, Diefenbaker attends the dedication of Diefenbaker Lake, an artificial body of water created by two dams, the larger of which has been named after Jimmy Gardiner.

At the PC party leadership convention in Toronto on September 9, a small army of bagpipers leads the Diefenbakers in; Robert Stanfield wins the leadership in the first ballot and Diefenbaker places fifth.

In Britain, Winston Churchill dies.

In France, Charles De Gaulle wins his second seventeen-year term as president of France.

1966
In Canada, the Medical Care Act is passed.

Indira Gandhi becomes prime minister of India.

1967
Canada celebrates the 100th birthday of Confederation; Expo 67 opens in Montreal as part of the festivities; De Gaulle visits Canada and shouts "_Vive le Québec libre!_" in Montreal.

The Six-Day War between Israel and Arab nations takes place.

In Washington, D.C., fifty thousand people demonstrate against the Vietnam war.

DIEFENBAKER AND HIS TIMES

1968
Now a loner on the Opposition side of the house, Diefenbaker disapproves of Prime Minister Trudeau's eccentric manner of dress.

In the June election Diefenbaker holds on to his seat; the PC party wins twenty-five fewer seats than when he was leader.

1972
In the general election, Diefenbaker campaigns using a helicopter; he wins his seat.

1974
Because Olive is sick, Diefenbaker campaigns without her by his side.

1976
Olive Diefenbaker, having suffered a stroke earlier, dies of a heart attack; her funeral is on Christmas Eve in Ottawa.

CANADA AND THE WORLD

1968
Pierre Elliott Trudeau succeeds Pearson as leader of the Liberal party and prime minister of Canada; he calls a June election; "Trudeaumania" takes the country by storm; Canada becomes officially bilingual; René Lévesque founds the Parti Québécois.

Civil rights leader Martin Luther King and presidential candidate Robert Kennedy are assassinated in the U.S.

1969
American astronaut Neil Armstrong is the first man to walk on the moon.

1970
In Canada, Prime Minister Trudeau invokes the War Measures Act during the FLQ crisis.

1972
In Canada, Trudeau retains power in a general election only by enlisting the support of the NDP for his minority government.

1974
In Canada, the Trudeau Liberals win a majority in the general election.

1976
In Canada, a divided PC party convention chooses Joe Clark as leader; in Quebec, the separatist Parti Québécois is elected under

DIEFENBAKER AND HIS TIMES	CANADA AND THE WORLD

CANADA AND THE WORLD

René Lévesque; Canada abolishes hanging for all but a few offences.

1978

In April, Diefenbaker accepts the nomination once more in Prince Albert; he receives a standing ovation.

1979

During the general election campaign, he suffers a stroke during the night; after several days he recovers and returns to campaigning; he wins by 4200 votes; he takes his seat in late July and on August 16 dies in his study at the age of eighty-three.

Diefenbaker's body lies in state for three days in the Hall of Honour of the Parliament Buildings; ten thousand people file past the open casket in Ottawa; a train takes his body to Prince Albert, then Saskatoon, where he lies in state at Convocation Hall of the University of Saskatchewan; he and Olive are buried beside the right Honourable John G. Diefenbaker Centre at the University of Saskatchewan.

1979

In Canada, Clark's PC party wins a minority government in May; Clark is the youngest prime minister ever and the first native westerner to hold the office; his decision to rule as if he has a majority is a mistake and his government falls on a vote of non-confidence in the budget.

1980

The Trudeau Liberals return to power; in Quebec, 60 per cent of the electorate vote in favour of unity with the rest of Canada.

Acknowledgments and Recommended Further Reading

No book is written alone, and this is especially true of a biography. People always wander in and give you a bit of information at the right time or point you in a direction you hadn't thought of before. I'd like to specifically thank three of those people: Rhonda Bailey, the editor of this book, for taking a chance on a fiction writer, and Dave Margoshes and Ven Begamudré for their advice. And a special nod of appreciation goes to Hugh Arscott for reading and commenting on this book. I discovered that everyone (and I mean everyone) has a Diefenbaker story. I want to thank all those people who shared theirs; it helped me understand how the Chief became a part of the national consciousness. And finally, thanks to my wife, Brenda Baker, for putting up with my musings about Diefenbaker. Yes, at times I became a Diefenbore.

There is no shortage of material on the life of John George Diefenbaker. In writing this book, I read and re-read Diefenbaker's *One Canada: Memoirs of The Right Honourable John G. Diefenbaker* (Toronto: Macmillan, 1972). I want to thank Carolyn Weir for granting permission to quote from these books. This three-volume memoir, written near the end of his life, was an inspiring view into the inner workings of Diefenbaker's personality. Equally inspiring, and daunting in its scope, was Denis Smith's *Rogue Tory: The Life and Legend of John*

G. Diefenbaker (Toronto: Macfarlane, Walter and Ross, 1995). This biography is one of the few that spans Diefenbaker's entire lifetime. I also wish to thank The University of Toronto Press for permission to quote from Peter Stursberg's *Diefenbaker: Leadership Lost 1962-67*. And finally I made many repeat visits to the Right Honourable John G. Diefenbaker Centre here in Saskatoon, where the staff was extremely helpful with my requests for information and photos (and for that I am thankful). At the Centre you can see the famous blue marlin and many other items from Diefenbaker's day. And for fun and more information about Dief, visit Diefenbakerweb at http://www.ggower.com/dief/. Finally, if there was a soundtrack for this book it would be scored by Bob Bossin, whose "Dief Will Be The Chief Again" was a #1 hit in Prince Albert in 1974. Visit Bob at http://www.island.net/~oldfolk/

What follows is a list of other books that were also helpful:

DONALDSON, Gordon. *Eighteen Men: The Prime Ministers of Canada*. Toronto: Doubleday Canada Limited, 1985.

HOLT, Simma. *The Other Mrs. Diefenbaker: A Biography of Edna Mae Brower*. Toronto: Doubleday, 1982.

MCILROY, Thad. (ed.) *Personal Letters of a Public Man: The Family Letters of John G. Diefenbaker*. Toronto: Doubleday, 1985.

NASH, Knowlton. *Kennedy and Diefenbaker: Fear and Loathing Across an Undefended Border*. Toronto: McClelland and Stewart, 1990.

NEWMAN, Peter C. *Renegade in Power: The Diefenbaker Years*. Toronto: McClelland and Stewart, 1963.

SPENCER, Dick. *Trumpets and Drums: John Diefenbaker on the Campaign Trail*. Toronto: Douglas & McIntyre, 1994.

STURSBERG, Peter. *Diefenbaker: Leadership Gained, 1956-1962*. Toronto: University of Toronto Press, 1975.

STURSBERG, Peter. *Diefenbaker: Leadership Lost, 1962-1967*. Toronto: University of Toronto Press, 1976.

WEIR, Carolyn. *The Right Honourable John George Diefenbaker: A Pictorial Tribute*. Toronto: The Macmillan Company of Canada, 1979.

WILSON, Garrett and Kevin WILSON. *Diefenbaker for the Defence*. Toronto: James Lorimar and Co., 1988.

VAN DUSEN, Thomas. *The Chief*. Toronto: McGraw Hill, 1968.

Index

*Printed in April 2001
at AGMV/Marquis,
Cap-Saint-Ignace (Québec).*